AN EXEMPLARY COUPLE

SAINT GIANNA BERETTA *and* PIETRO MOLLA

AN EXEMPLARY COUPLE

SAINT GIANNA BERETTA *and* PIETRO MOLLA

Their Marital Journey and Message Today

VALENTINA DI MARCO

TAN Books
Gastonia, North Carolina

This work was first published in Italian in the year 2022 by Editrice Velar.

Cover design by Jordan Avery

Cover image: Saint Gianna with Pietro during their honeymoon at Taormina, Messina, Italy, October 1955.

Cover and interior images are from the Pietro Molla Photo Archive

ISBN: 978-1-5051-3262-5
Kindle ISBN: 978-1-5051-3464-3
ePUB ISBN: 978-1-5051-3465-0

Published in the United States by
TAN Books
PO Box 269
Gastonia, NC 28053
www.TANBooks.com

Printed in India

Dedicated to my parents Paolo and Lucia.

Saint Gianna,
help us to pray for a better world
where the family returns to being
the point of reference
to overcome life's adversities.

Contents

Foreword

In every age of human history, God raises up holy men and women to light the way and inspire us to holiness of life during the days of our earthly pilgrimage with its true destiny: eternal life. Valentina Di Marco's book, written originally in Italian and now published in English translation, *An Exemplary Couple: Saint Gianna Beretta and Pietro Molla. Their Marital Journey and Message Today*, offers a striking literary portrait of this saintly couple to inspire us, especially the married, on the daily pilgrimage to our lasting home in Heaven. The book, with remarkable simplicity, presents the profound nature of the marital vocation, relationship, and life of Saint Gianna Beretta Molla and her saintly husband Pietro Molla. The author, in her study to prepare the writing of the book, was blessed to enjoy the counsel of her learned mentor Monsignor Ennio Apeciti who has the care of the Service of the Causes of Saints in the Archdiocese of Milan. She also drew great inspiration from the intimate and heartfelt witness of Dr. Gianna Emanuela Molla, M.D., the youngest child of Saint Gianna and Pietro Molla.

The book begins with a brief biographical section that includes new details about the lives of the saintly couple, especially in their families of origin. It is particularly rich in details about the life of Pietro Molla, which have not been included in previous publications. Pietro, who was a truly humble man, kept his personal life hidden as he generously shared as much as possible the details of the life of his saintly wife. As a widower, he steadfastly devoted all his energy, first, to being a good father for his young children who had lost their mother in death, and then, to carrying out with excellence his service as an engineer of the renowned S.A.F.F.A. Company [*Società per Azioni Fabbriche Fiammiferi e Affini*—Company for the Fabrication of Matches and Related Products].

Exploring the rich correspondence of Pietro and Gianna, Valentina Di Marco illustrates the deeply grounded spirituality of their spousal relationship. In studying the language of their very personal and moving letters, she presents the depth of their love for God, for the Blessed Virgin Mary, and for each other, their family, and their neighbor. Their correspondence, much of which has been published, is a testimony to the work of Divine Grace at work in their hearts as husband and wife, father and mother, for their eternal salvation and that of their children.

You have in your hands the fruits of Valentina Di Marco's study. She shows the virtues which marked the relationship of Pietro and Gianna, distinguishing three distinct time periods of their lives together: the time during their engagement, the time during their marriage, and the time of their parenting. In a wonderful way, she illustrates the goodness of their relationship through authoritative texts of the Church's Magisterium, especially as it is presented in the writings of the Roman Pontiffs. In each of the distinct times of their exemplary relationship we see a deep prayer life and an abiding trust in Divine Providence, whether in joyful times or in times of sorrow. We know well that they experienced many difficulties and much suffering in their life together, and that their response was always steadfast faith and trust in God and in His promises. In a particular way, the author shows how deep faith and hope sustained Pietro after the death of his beloved Gianna, as a young mother, and again, just two years after the death of Gianna, when his dear child Maria Zita, called Mariolina, died in her seventh year of life.

The author illustrates the couple's struggles, their genuine human fears and challenges, and their blessings—Pietro's as an engineer and Gianna's as a medical doctor—and their strengths derived especially from their communication with God through prayer, devotion, and the Sacraments, and from their heartfelt communication with each other. Saint Gianna and her saintly husband, Pietro, are contemporary heroes of the much-needed New Evangelization—living in Christ with new energy and new enthusiasm like His first disciples—promoted by Pope Saint John Paul II, especially in what pertains to the inviolability of innocent and defenseless human life, and the integrity of marriage and family as the cradle of human life. Reading the book, we understand how they fulfilled the call of the married to be the instruments of each other's sanctification. We see how recognizing their own dependance upon God and upon each other, they relied upon each other and received strength from each other.

Enjoying the fruits of Valentina Di Marco's study, we see how the solemnly declared heroic sanctity of Saint Gianna had everything to do with the holiness of life of her husband Pietro. Both Pietro and Gianna, as every married couple should be, were dedicated to work for the salvation of the spouse's soul. Of special note is how the excellent study of the author opens a view into the dimensions of Pietro's holiness of life. Indeed, his sacrifices and generosity, as well as his hard work on the Cause of Beatification and Canonization of Saint Gianna, enabled the world to know the most beautiful story—in all its rich details—of the life of his beloved spouse, Saint Gianna. How much more we can learn about their life as a couple now that we also have his story, beautifully woven together with that of his wife, a canonized saint. We need the example of married love, of marital fidelity and lifelong sacrifice today more than ever. Saint Gianna and Pietro Molla are truly examples for our time.

We live in a world in which the supreme goods of marriage and the family, and human life are so little known and so often violated. In stark contrast, Pietro and Gianna bring to the world a powerful testimony to the faithful, enduring, and lifegiving love of marriage. Their testimony inspires hope and renewed commitment to the family as the foundation of the life of all society. Their story can inspire a conversion of life in those who are inattentive and careless in fulfilling the wonderful call to the married life.

With these important considerations in mind, I express heartfelt gratitude to Valentina Di Marco for her in-depth study of the heroically holy couple Pietro Molla and Gianna Beretta Molla. May her account of their exemplary holiness inspire us all to recognize and respect more fully the union of man and woman in marriage in accord with God's plan for our salvation and for the salvation of the world.

RAYMOND LEO CARDINAL BURKE
May 31, 2024.

Gianna with Pierluigi, near her car, 1957.

INTRODUCTION

"From Bernate I went to Cascina Crespi, because I was called for a medical visit, and then I went to Mesero."[1]

THIS phrase is taken from one of the numerous letters that Saint Gianna Beretta, a pediatrician, exchanged with her husband, engineer Pietro Molla. Apparently, this would seem to be an insignificant excerpt, the chronicle of an ordinary working day, no different from all the others; the letter does not go into further detail, but what emerges is the availability of a doctor always present when called for a medical visit. If this excerpt seems not very significant, or even insignificant, to most people, to this writer, this phrase is a herald of confirmations, gratitude, and inspirations for the following work.

The mentioned "*Cascina Crespi*" is a cottage situated on a country road connecting Mesero (Pietro Molla's birthplace, where Dr. Beretta's medical office was located, and where today both Gianna and Pietro rest in the cemetery's family chapel) and Casate, the small hamlet of Bernate Ticino where this writer has always lived. In the "*Cascina Crespi,*" populated by several families, the family of my grandparents Pietro and Annetta also lived, with their children Antonio, Cristina, and Luigi; my father Paolo was born there on November 12, 1954, thanks to the intervention of Dr. Beretta. Saint

[1] Letter of 14 December 1955, in Gianna Beretta. Pietro Molla, *Lettere*, edited by E. Guerriero, Ed. San Paolo, Cinisello Balsamo (Milan) 2012, p. 108. A new edition of the work was printed by Cantagalli Publishers in 2023.

Gianna was the doctor who took care of my family, and a friend of my grandmother; she helped her during her penultimate uncompleted pregnancy and her last one, which gave birth to my father; she was also the doctor of my uncles and my father. My uncles still remember when, in case of need, they rushed to the main road to stop her car and divert it towards their cottage; they often recall how she always complimented my grandmother for the beauty, in particular, of my uncle Luigi, and how she always said: "*If I will have a son, I'll call him Luigi.*" Gianna and Pietro's firstborn indeed took the name Pierluigi, in homage to his paternal grandfather, as their daughter Gianna Emanuela, whom I have had the pleasure to know, has confirmed.

Then, Saint Gianna has been part of my family history; a family that is not native to these areas, but that is the fruit of a Abruzzese (from the Abruzzo Region) "*carabiniere*" (a kind of Italian policeman) grandfather and of a saintly Piemontese grandmother transplanted to the Lombard countryside.

In December 1955, when the letter was written from which the excerpt above is taken, my paternal family was still living at "*Cascina Crespi,*" before moving to nearby Casate; it is not possible to know whom Saint Gianna went to visit that day, but I like to think that she might have gone to cure a disease of my father and his brothers.

As a result of these "family" reflections, it seemed natural therefore to dedicate my Master's thesis in Religious Sciences to Saint Gianna.

The area that has been chosen to study in depth is more strictly biographical; I got married on May 31, 2013. As the theme of vocation, engagement, marriage, and family became increasingly important in my personal experience, I wanted to study it in depth through an exceptional document: the letters exchanged between Saint Gianna and her husband, Pietro.

It is a correspondence that is worth as much as the Magisterium of the popes and the Church because it is the simple putting into practice of the teaching of Jesus. The letters express, with a language that is at times very poetic, all the love that, right from the start, united Gianna and Pietro, their purposes, their total dedication to the other and to the vocation of family. They are letters that exude joy, while facing the daily difficulties of every day and every family.

The publication of these letters makes it possible to enter the private life and the deepest feelings of a man and a woman who have been able to love until the end, in the absolute respect of the other and in the will to give and defend the precious and inestimable gift of life.

Faced with the objection of those who say that Gianna Beretta was canonized for a gesture (setting aside her own life to defend and save her daughter's) that many other less "famous" mothers would have done, and have done, it would be enough to read only a few passages of these letters. In this correspondence is set down, in black and white, the most significant part of a life totally lived on the teaching of the Gospel, also in the primary sphere of one's personal vocation.

It is a practical demonstration of how holiness can be lived even in everyday life, in the normal things of life, and, in particular, in married life, as Cardinal Martini reminded young people participating in Spiritual Exercises in the Cathedral at the conclusion of Gianna's beatification process:[2]

> *"The testimonials say: she was a very normal woman, who practiced her profession as a doctor very well; she was an excellent mother; she liked being in the world; she radiated joy and enthusiasm around her. But her confidence in Providence was very strong."*[3]

---

2 21 March 1986.

3 E. Apeciti, *Voci di Chiesa per santa Gianna*, Centro Ambrosiano, Milan 2004, pp. 29–30.

This work begins with a brief biographical presentation of the protagonists, Gianna and Pietro, and with the chronicle, through direct testimonies, of the most significant moments of their married life: their engagement time, marriage, the conception of parenthood, and their experience as parents.

An effort has then been made to analyze their marital journey through their correspondence, bringing out the distinctive features of their relationship as fiancés, spouses, and parents; in each stage, the most significant and, perhaps, curious characteristics have been emphasized.

A fundamental characteristic immediately emerges: the great personality and spirituality of Pietro Molla. The joyful and profound faith of Saint Gianna, her gifts as a young person involved in Catholic Action, as a doctor at the service of neighbor, as a wife in love and as an attentive mother, have always been talked about; since the year of his death (in 2010), the figure of the engineer Pietro Molla, the worthy spouse of a holy woman, has also begun to be studied in depth.

Gianna and Pietro in London, 1961.

In the final part of this work, we wanted to compare what emerged from the daily spirituality of the Beretta-Molla spouses with the texts of the Magisterium and the messages of the Popes regarding engagement, marriage, prayer in the family, work, and parenthood. What emerges is how much Gianna and Pietro are both the forerunners and the embodiment of the magisterium that followed them.

In the conclusions, an effort has been made to highlight how Gianna and Pietro, through their marital journey, can be an example and can convey their message even today, in a society in which marriage and the family are continually diminished and denigrated.

1
Gianna Beretta

"When Gianna passed away, only her sacrifice was known. Bishop Carlo Colombo himself, in the letter sent to her brother in which he invited him to collect some testimonies, spoke of extraordinary sacrifice; after all, he did not know Gianna's whole life. So initially we thought of the extraordinary gesture of a martyr. Then, when her life was examined, and Gianna's writings were read and studied, we then realized that Gianna's whole life was an uninterrupted gesture of Christian witness, of grace. Then, it was this deepening that led to the final image of a woman, of a mother beatified precisely for the way in which she was able to live all the phases of her life."[4]

AS also pointed out in the testimony of her husband, Pietro Molla, for a long time Gianna Beretta was remembered only for the final choice of her life: to continue with her pregnancy to give birth to the baby girl she was carrying in her womb, and, therefore, to put her life at the highest risk. In September 1961, at the start of a new pregnancy, a large fibroid was found in her uterus; her brother Ferdinando (called Nando), a medical doctor, recalls:

---

[4] P. Molla - E. Guerriero, *Gianna la donna forte. La beata Gianna Beretta Molla nel ricordo del marito*, Ed. San Paolo, Cinisello Balsamo (Milan) 1995, p. 92. A new edition of the work was printed by Cantagalli Publishers in 2024.

> *"While I was examining her, I immediately realized that a large fibroid was growing next to her uterus which, among other things, was beginning to cause her intestinal colics that in a short time would have become more and more painful. I therefore had her urgently re-examined by Professor Mario Vitali, chief gynecologist of the hospital in Monza, who confirmed my diagnosis and recommended a timely operation."*[5]

Before the surgery to remove the fibroids, precisely because she was a doctor and aware of the risks, Gianna begged the surgeon to save her baby in any case.

Her brother Ferdinando himself writes this in the clinical report drawn up after the operation at which he had assisted:

> *"[. . .] Before the operation, in the presence of Professor Vitali, her husband and myself, the patient did not hesitate to put the life of her creature before her own, [. . .] and she begged the surgeon to be inspired, during his surgery, by this desire of hers."*[6]

The surgery seemed successful, but on the eve of giving birth Gianna remained convinced to put the new life before her own. She told her husband Pietro, "*in a firm and at the same time serene tone of voice, with a profound gaze that he will never forget:*

> *'If you must decide between me and the baby, do not hesitate: choose—and I demand it—the baby. Do save the baby.'*[7]

Pietro, who knew the thoughtfulness and the strength of his wife's decisions well, felt obliged in conscience to respect Gianna's will,

---

5 G. Pelucchi, *L'amore più grande. Santa Gianna Beretta Molla*, Ed. Paoline, Milan 2004, p. 132.

6 *Ibid.*, p. 133.

7 *Santa Gianna Beretta Molla: Una Vita per la Vita*, edited by G. E. Molla, Ed. Fondazione Santa Gianna Beretta Molla, Mesero (Milan) - Associazione Amici di Santa Gianna Beretta Molla, Magenta (Milan) 2010, p. 14.

although aware of the possible painful consequences for his family. But Gianna was convinced that the new baby had the same rights as the other three children, Pierluigi (born November 19, 1956), Maria Zita called Mariolina (born December 11, 1957, who died on February 12, 1964, of acute glomerulonephritis), and Laura (July 15, 1959). She also knew that she was the only means of Providence to bring that baby into the world. For the education and raising of the children Gianna relied on Providence, her husband, and their relatives. On the morning of April 21, 1962, Holy Saturday, Gianna gave birth by caesarean section to little Gianna Emanuela at the San Gerardo Hospital in Monza. However, her condition worsened with fever and excruciating abdominal pains caused by septic peritonitis. Her ordeal then began, assisted by some relatives and her sister Virginia, a Canossian nun who had inexplicably and providentially returned from a mission in India.

> *"I returned by chance to Italy, from the mission, just in time to see her again . . . I had not been well and in India my superiors had sent me for a rest in the mountains to recover. While I was up there, I thought that perhaps I could ask Mother General for permission to return to my home in Magenta. [. . .] It seemed that Mother General's permission would never come. Finally, one day, I learned that I could leave. Immediately, some officials who knew us facilitated the necessary papers and found me a place on the first ship that sailed for Italy and, fortunately, this ship reached Italy in only eleven days instead of the usual fifteen. Without this unexpected speed, I would have arrived after my sister's death."*[8]

Mother Virginia recalls those moments, once she arrived at the bedside of her sister, with whom she had always had a strong bond:

---

[8] G. Pelucchi, *L'amore più grande. Santa Gianna Beretta Molla*, Ed. Paoline, Milan 2004, p. 32.

> *"She refused any sedative, in order to always be conscious and aware of what was happening. Not only that, but also so that she could be lucid in her relationship with her Jesus, whom she constantly invoked."*[9]

Despite the treatments, her condition worsened. Her brother Ferdinando had accepted from Gianna the task of alerting her with a predetermined phrase when the time of her death was imminent. Lacking the courage to do so, he asked Mother Virginia, her sister, to tell her:

> *"Have courage, Gianna, Dad and Mom are in Heaven waiting for you—are you happy to go there?"*[10]

Mother Virginia also recalls:

> *"In the movement of her eyelash one could read her complete and loving adherence to the Divine Will, even if veiled by the pain of having to leave her beloved children who were still so small. Gianna, like her Jesus, gave herself up to the Father."*[11]

At dawn on April 28, as she wished and had previously asked of Pietro, Gianna was brought back to her home in Ponte Nuovo di Magenta, where she died at 8 a.m. She was only thirty-nine. Her heroic choice recalls Jesus's sacrifice on the cross, but above all crowns an entire existence based on Christian principles and on following the Gospel message in her vocation as doctor, wife, and mother, and as an active participant of the Church through Catholic Action. Only an in-depth examination of her biography revealed a complete

---

9 *Santa Gianna Beretta Molla: Una Vita per la Vita*, edited by G. E. Molla, Ed. Fondazione Santa Gianna Beretta Molla, Mesero (Milan) - Associazione Amici di Santa Gianna Beretta Molla, Magenta (Milan) 2010, p. 14.

10 *Ibid.*, p. 15.

11 *Ibid.*, p. 15.

Christian woman, who shows how holiness can be achieved by every baptized person also in the vocation of work and marriage.

> *"In our own days too the Church is constantly enriched by the witness of the many women who fulfil their vocation to holiness. Holy women are an incarnation of the feminine ideal; they are also a model for all Christians, a model of the "sequela Christi," an example of how the Bride must respond with love to the love of the Bridegroom."*[12]

Gianna was a woman fully integrated in her time, at the forefront of thought and action: beautiful and intelligent, cultured and a convicted Christian. Always well-dressed and well-groomed, she wore the jewels given by her husband without affectation. She painted, had a driver's license (unusual in the 1940s and 50s) and loved music, theatrical performances, and outdoor sports:

> *"She knew how to enjoy the beautiful things in life; she liked art and music; she was a mountain climber and a very good skier. She was very elegant, liked to dress well, and she knew how to enjoy the beautiful things that the Eternal Father gives us."*[13]

In one of her early letters to her husband, Gianna herself testifies, especially, to her love for the mountains and skiing:

> *"I get up at 8 o'clock in the morning (how lazy! by then you're already at the office!) because at 8:30 a.m. there is Holy Mass. [. . .] After breakfast, we immediately set off on our skis and down . . . the slopes. At 11, I usually take lessons with the ski instructor and . . . modesty aside, I have learned to make even*

[12] *Mulieris Dignitatem*, no. 27.

[13] From the interview with her son Pierluigi Molla on the occasion of the VII World Meeting of Families, held from May 30–June 3, 2012 in Milan http://www.youtube.com/watch?v=F5SQ06KaZ_I.

> *difficult descents. But do not worry, there is no danger because where the descent is too steep the teacher makes you go down the easiest way."*[14]

Gianna's well-groomed, elegant, and extremely jovial appearance can be also seen from the numerous photographs available. She is one of the first saints of whom we have images taken from everyday life.

A few weeks before her fourth delivery, after which she lost her life, Gianna sought to entertain herself with fashion magazines to forget her anxieties (albeit hidden from her husband and family) regarding the difficult pregnancy; in fact, Pietro mentions it:

> *"[...] the two fashion magazines you had me buy in Paris, where I had to go for work in March 1962, when you said to me: 'If the Lord keeps me here, I want to let off some steam!'"*[15]

Gianna's inner strength not only transformed into spiritual and apostolic commitment but also into energy for fun activities.

> *"My wife, for example, loved and practiced sports: she played tennis, skied, and went mountain climbing. Another memory dear to me is that of dancing. Gianna knew how to dance well. The last time I danced with her at the Grand Hotel in Stockholm in 1961 she was admired by those present. She, therefore, had a full, overflowing life."*[16]

---

14 Letter of 23 March 1955, in Gianna Beretta. Pietro Molla, *Lettere*, edited by E. Guerriero, Ed. San Paolo, Cinisello Balsamo (Milan) 2012, pp. 73-74.

15 From the testimony of Pietro Molla in *Gianna Sorriso di a Dio,* quarterly Publication edited by Fondazione Santa Gianna Beretta Molla, Year 3 no. 8, December 2004, p. 1.

16 P. Molla - E. Guerriero, *Gianna la donna forte. La beata Gianna Beretta Molla nel ricordo del marito,* Ed. San Paolo, Cinisello Balsamo (Milan) 1995, p. 53.

The Family of Origin

Giovanna Francesca Beretta was born on October 4, 1922 (the feast of Saint Francis of Assisi) in Magenta (Milan) in the country house of her paternal grandparents (in the current Via Roma 89) and was baptized in the Basilica of San Martino on the 11th of the same month by her paternal uncle, Fr. Giuseppe. She was the tenth of thirteen children, five of whom died in infancy (Davide, Rosina, and Pierina were killed by the Spanish flu; Guglielmina and Anna Maria died very young). Three of her siblings consecrated themselves to God.

The secret of Gianna's holiness seems to lie precisely in her family of origin; as her husband Pietro recalls,

> *"Gianna had the immeasurable gift of deeply and exemplary Christian parents."*[17]

Her parents, Franciscan Third Order members, were known for their simple and great faith. They were married on October 12, 1908, in the church of San Bartolomeo in Milan.

Alberto Beretta (1881–1942), her father, was an old-fashioned man, "*he spoke little and thought a lot*" as his son Fr. Giuseppe recalls.[18] He lost his mother at the age of four and attended school as a boarding student at the Diocesan *Collegio San Carlo* in Milan. He worked at the Cantoni cotton mill for thirty-eight years and made great sacrifices to allow all his children to study until graduation, by reducing useless expenses, like when out of the blue he quit smoking cigars.

All the children rewarded their father's efforts by obtaining brilliant results in their educational and professional careers: Amalia, called Iucci, was a pianist but died at the age of only twenty-seven. Francesco

---

17 E. Apeciti, *Gianna Beretta Molla. Amare la vita,* Centro Ambrosiano, Milan 2004, p. 16.

18 *Ibid.*, p. 16.

became an engineer, as did Giuseppe, who also became a priest; Zita was a pharmacist; Ferdinando and Gianna became doctors, as did Virginia, who became a Canossian missionary nun; and Enrico, who became a Capuchin missionary priest with the name of Father Alberto Maria. In this regard, Cardinal Carlo Maria Martini wrote:

> *"I am impressed by the fact that Gianna and her siblings have all achieved prestigious professional qualifications: two engineers, four doctors, a pharmacist, and a concert performer. These results certainly reward each one's intellectual gifts and earnest efforts, also reflecting the economic possibilities and the wise administration of the family's assets. But I believe that their parents' way of listening to them was a determining factor."*[19]

Maria De Micheli (1887–1942), her mother, was the eldest of five daughters, and from a young age, she had thought of entering the religious life, but then she dedicated herself entirely to family. She went to Mass every morning with her husband and children and was close to each of her children, even learning Latin and Greek so she could follow them better in their studies. A skilled seamstress, she personally made clothes for all her children.

Here is a glimpse of daily family life offered by Fr. Giuseppe Beretta, Gianna's brother:

> *"Mom was truly the strong woman spoken of in the Scriptures. Her day began early, at 5 o'clock, when dad got up to go to early Mass and begin his day's work before the Lord and in the name of the Lord. He went to Mass alone, because mom stayed home to prepare breakfast for him, and his lunch she put in a briefcase.*
>
> *After dad left for his workplace in Milan, mom came to our little bedrooms and, touching our face lightly with her hand, woke us up. We knew that she would soon go to church*

[19] C. M. Martini, *Una famiglia così,* Centro Ambrosiano, Milan 1994, p. 23.

to attend Holy Mass, and we dressed in a hurry, happy to kneel next to her to prepare ourselves to receive Jesus in Holy Communion and make our thanksgiving with her. What wonderful words she suggested to us to say to Jesus! Then, back home, we had breakfast, and then off to school.

Mom, after having tidied up the house and made our beds, sat down on her armchair with a large basket full of linen to sew and mend, and of socks to patch up next to her. She never complained, she was always smiling, and she never seemed tired. With all the work she had, she found time to do also some meditation from a booklet entitled 'The Gift of Self' by a French author. Later on, one day it came into my hands and reading it I felt like I was seeing my mom who had so deeply meditated upon it and translated its pages into her demeanor. [. . .]

And dad? A man of few words, but those few were the fruit of reflection and wisdom. He was certainly not secondary in faith and piety to our mother: a gentleman whom you could trust with your eyes closed. He came home in the evening from Milan, and two or three of us went to meet him at the arrival station of the Città Alta[20] *funicular to carry his briefcase, and with our chatter we erased the signs of fatigue from his face. He had only to cross the threshold of the house, meet our mom's smile and the cheerful welcome of all his children to regain all his serenity. It was dinner time, and everything was already ready. After a short prayer, we sat happily at that long table. How nice it is to be so many siblings around our parents!*

He liked to hear a bit from everyone about how school had gone, and when some pranks occurred, he frowned in a way to make us understand without many words that it should not happen again. After dinner, while dad smoked his cigar, our older sister Amalia, a skilled piano player, had us listen and

---

[20] This refers to the period from 1925 to 1937, when the Beretta family lived in Bergamo.

enjoy the most beautiful pieces by Chopin, Bach, and Beethoven. Then came another important moment in our family life, that of the recitation of the Holy Rosary. Dad would stand before the image of Our Lady with the older children next to him, and we younger ones around our mom, who helped us to respond until we fell asleep resting on her knees."[21]

As emerges from this testimony, the typical day of the Beretta family was marked by prayer and participation in the Eucharist.

Alberto and Maria died within four months of each other:

"They were two extraordinary people, who complemented each other perfectly. They loved each other very much. Just think that when they got married, they had recited a prayer in which they asked God to die together. They could not imagine their life separated from each other. And this prayer was answered: on April 28, 1942, my dad told my mom that he felt very poorly. 'I'm dying, Maria,' he insisted with anguish. My mom looked at him carefully for a moment and: 'That's not possible,' she replied to him. 'I'm very well. I don't feel anything.' But, just on the evening of the same day, my mom had a heart attack and died the following day."[22]

The Berettas were a rather wealthy family but did not flaunt wealth and managed money wisely, always offering their help to the needy.

Until 1924, Gianna lived in Milan, in Piazza Risorgimento 10; the family attended the church of the Capuchin Convent in Viale Piave.

---

21 Giuseppe Beretta, *The roots of a holiness*, in *Terra Ambrosiana,* bi-monthly Publication of the Diocese of Milan, year XXXXV, no. 1 January–February 1994, pp. 33–34.

22 G. Pelucchi, *L'amore più grande. Santa Gianna Beretta Molla,* Ed. Paoline, Milan 2004, pp. 25–26.

Youth

Little Gianna decisively welcomed the gift of faith and the Christian education of her parents. In Bergamo, where her family had moved in Borgo Canale (a borough of Bergamo) in 1925 because of the Spanish flu epidemic, she received her First Holy Communion (at the age of five, in the Provost Parish of Saint Grata *inter vites*) and her Confirmation (at the age of eight, in the Cathedral). She attended the first- and second-year class at the Elementary School of Colle Aperto, the third-year class at the Sisters of La Sagesse, and the fourth and fifth at the Institute of the Canossian Sisters in Via Sudorno. In 1933 she began her first high school year at "Paolo Sarpi," State Classic High School. In 1937, the year in which her older sister Amalia died, she moved to Genova Quinto a Mare where she attended the Institute of Santa Dorotea and matured in her faith thanks also to the Spiritual Exercises preached (from March 16 to 18, 1938), by Jesuit Father Michele Avedano.

Worried about her health, her parents decided to make her take a year off by suspending her studies; Gianna had the opportunity to increase her commitment to Catholic Action, collaborating in particular with Monsignor Mario Righetti. In October 1939 she began studies at the Classical High School of the Dorothean Sisters.

In 1942, she lost both her parents a few months apart (her mother on April 29 and her father on September 10); she received her high school diploma (in June) and moved with her siblings to their paternal grandparents' home in Magenta; she enrolled in the School of Medicine and Surgery, first at the Milan University and then in Pavia, where she took a degree in 1949, becoming one of the few professional women at that time.

Along with her sisters, she joined the life of the parish of San Martino, and she worked both for the education of youth in the youth club of the Canossian Sisters and for the needy in the Conferences of the Dames of St. Vincent de Paul.

Gianna (the first from the left), her mother, Virginia, Amalia, her father; Francesco (behind Gianna), Ferdinando, Zita, Enrico (Father Alberto), and Giuseppe, on the day of the 25th anniversary of her parents' wedding, Bergamo, October 12th, 1933.

In 1950, she opened a medical office for INAM patients (Istituto Nazionale per l'Assicurazione contro le Malattie—National Institute for Insurance against Diseases) in Mesero and substituted, if it was necessary, for her brother Doctor, Ferdinando in Magenta.

In 1952 she specialized in pediatrics and (from 1956) took on various positions within the schools of the area (in Ponte Nuovo), including working for free.

She had a predilection for the elderly, children, and mothers, convinced of her mission as a doctor and that: ". . . *just as he (the priest) can touch Jesus, so we (doctors) touch Jesus in the body of our sick: the poor, the young, the old, and children.*"

As Pietro recalls:

> *"Gianna soon became familiar to everyone with her (car) Fiat 600 that reached even the most isolated and far from the city*

center farmhouses. [. . .] How many children did Gianna treat, and how many mothers did she encourage and advise!"[23]

Her son Pierluigi also testified, on the occasion of the International Theological Pastoral Congress of the VII World Meeting of Families (in Milan) held on May 31, 2012 at the Congress Center of the De Filippi Collegio in Varese during the afternoon dedicated to the theme "Professional freedom and family life":

" [. . .] Recalling the figure of my mother instead I see a person who was already modern at the time, who, although firmly anchored to traditional values, was an example of a woman who had been able to combine work and family with mastery, but above all naturalness."[24]

Gianna wondered and prayed about her vocation; from the exchange of letters with her Capuchin brother, Father Alberto, who spoke of the work he had to face in the mission, she reached the decision to join him in Grajaú, in the State of Maranhão in Brazil, to help him as a lay missionary.

Father Alberto, with the help of his engineer brother Francesco, was, in fact, building a modern hospital; to prepare herself for departure, Gianna attended the Mangiagalli Obstetric Clinic in Milan and studied Portuguese. She wrote to her brother:

"Dearest Father Alberto, [. . .] I am so very happy to come, and I think this is truly my vocation. I prayed, and for this purpose also, at the end of the month, I will go to do the Spiritual Exercises, so that the Lord may tell me yes or no."[25]

---

23 P. Molla - E. Guerriero, *Gianna la donna forte. La beata Gianna Beretta Molla nel ricordo del marito,* Ed. San Paolo, Cinisello Balsamo (Milan) 1995, p. 57.

24 From the testimony of her son Pierluigi in *Gianna Sorriso di Dio,* year 11, nos. 30–31–32, January–December 2012, p. 36.

25 Letter of 12 September 1952 of Gianna to her brother Father Alberto.

But her physical constitution was not robust and was ill-suited for the tropical heat; her family, her spiritual director, Msgr. Enrico Ceriani, and the Bishop of Bergamo, Msgr. Adriano Bernareggi (through her brother Fr. Giuseppe), convinced her that this was not her path. Curiously, her husband Pietro writes:

> *"If I had known before, with my character, I would never have been able to approach a girl who had such a thought."*[26]

Her sister, Mother Virginia, also testifies:

> *"After having accepted the advice of her Spiritual Director who had said to her: 'Why don't you also form a family, a holy one, like your family of origin, imitating the example of your parents?', Gianna joined our brother Ferdinando in June 1954 who left for Lourdes with a Unitalsi train (Italian National Union to Transport the Sick to Lourdes and International Sanctuaries) to accompany the sick, because she wanted to pray to Our Lady of Lourdes to let her meet the man who should be her spouse, whom the Lord had prepared for her from eternity."*[27]

The Lord, in fact, had another plan in store for Gianna, another vocation.

---

26 P. Molla - E. Guerriero, *Gianna la donna forte. La beata Gianna Beretta Molla nel ricordo del marito,* Ed. San Paolo, Cinisello Balsamo (Milan) 1995, p. 43.

27 Cf. *Gianna Sorriso di Dio,* year 7, no. 20, September–December 2008, p. 8.

2
Pietro Molla

"Two immeasurable gifts the good God has given us: a holy Mom in Heaven and an exemplary Dad on Earth."[28]

AT dawn on Holy Saturday, April 3, 2010, the engineer Pietro Molla died at his home in Mesero at the venerable age of almost ninety-eight.

His figure is extremely paradigmatic, the first case in the history of a spouse witnessing the process of canonization of the other. It was Pietro himself who recalled this:

> *"The other day I was in Reggio Emilia for a testimony about Gianna and I went to greet the Bishop who jokingly said to me: 'Molla, you are a unique case. When a man and a woman marry, they become one unique person, so half of you is already in Paradise, the other half is here with us.'"*[29]

This man, without opposing, but as a sacrifice, opened wide the doors of his life, his affections, his sorrows to give the world and the Church the figure of his holy wife. As his daughter Laura writes:

---

28 Letter posthumous from daughter Laura to her father in *Gianna Sorriso di Dio,* year 9, nos. 24–25–26, January–December 2010, p. 11.

29 P. Molla - E. Guerriero, *Gianna la donna forte. La beata Gianna Beretta Molla nel ricordo del marito,* Ed. San Paolo, Cinisello Balsamo (Milan) 1995, pp. 85-86.

> *"To fulfill the will of the Lord and to honor the memory of Mom, you accepted sharing with the whole World the splendid short earthly history that you have lived together."*[30]

But his astonishment for the Church's request and his hesitations in making public his marital and family life were expressed by Pietro himself, who right from the start analyzed the situation with intelligence and reservedness:

> *"In the spring of 1970 Bishop Carlo Colombo, who came to my parish in Ponte Nuovo of Magenta to administer Holy Confirmation, had me called to the parish house and communicated to me the desire of the Church - eight years had already passed since Gianna had died - to promote the cause of beatification of my wife, and he asked me for my approval. I was very surprised! I had never heard of a woman, a mother of a family, made a saint. 'Think about it,' I told him. 'I didn't realize that I lived next to a saint.'*
>
> *My reluctance came from the fact that I immediately understood that this meant making public our life, our affections, our sufferings. [. . .] Some mothers could have understood her sacrifice, while others would have considered it an exhibition, almost a provocation. I was also afraid of the press; we have always been a bit reserved."*[31]

The children were small, and Pietro had to decide by himself. The eldest, Pierluigi, recalls:

> *"We were not involved in the decision because of our age. I think, however, knowing dad, that he accepted that decision out of love and respect for the life and the choices of Mom,*

---

[30] Letter posthumous from daughter Laura to her father in *Gianna Sorriso di Dio,* year 9, nos. 24–25–26, January–December 2010, p. 11.

[31] P. Molla - E. Guerriero, *Gianna la donna forte. La beata Gianna Beretta Molla nel ricordo del marito,* Ed. San Paolo, Cinisello Balsamo (Milan) 1995, p. 77.

convinced that through his 'not opposing' he would have honored the memory and the remembrance of his adored spouse."[32]

The father himself, Pietro, confirms:

> *"I was particularly struck by Monsignor Colombo's consideration that Gianna's witness could do so much good. [. . .] A negative answer seemed to me to be in striking contrast to that eagerness for apostolate, with that will to do good to her neighbor, to help the elderly and needy, which Gianna had always shown in her life."*[33]

The process of beatification and canonization, in its various phases by which Gianna passed from "servant of God" to "venerable" and then "blessed" and "saint," allowed Pietro himself to reconsider the life of his wife and know her spiritual depth.

Pietro, with Gianna Emanuela on his side, greets deeply moved Pope Saint John Paul II, St. Peter's Square, Rome, May 16th, 2004, day of Gianna's Canonization.

Banner with Gianna and Mariolina hanging from the balcony of St. Peter's Basilica.

---

[32] From the testimony of his son Pierluigi in *Gianna Sorriso di Dio,* year 9, nos. 24–25–26, January–December 2010, p. 10.

[33] P. Molla - E. Guerriero, *Gianna la donna forte. La beata Gianna Beretta Molla nel ricordo del marito,* Ed. San Paolo, Cinisello Balsamo (Milan) 1995, p. 78.

> *"I could also read Gianna's writings, which I did not know before. She, in fact, had not brought her writings at our home but had left them in her house in Magenta. Not only that, but in her usual discretion, in her unwillingness to 'let the right hand know what the left hand is doing,' she had never spoken to me of her very significant commitment to Catholic voluntary service."*[34]

In order to get to know Pietro Molla, it is possible to draw on the testimonies of people who knew him closely. His daughter Laura writes:

> *"With how much enthusiasm and incessant strength of will you have faced the many undertakings that life had in store for you. The "thirst" for knowledge and innovation that have always distinguished you have been a particular spur to me. Your facing up to problems with great diplomacy, your repeating: 'to postpone most of the time means not do,' your tireless work, as an executive, as a father, and as the main maker of the collection of the memories of Mom and of the spreading of her message in the World, your incessantly asking for help from the Lord and from Mom through prayer, have been for me a high example of life and action."*[35]

The person who has been closest to him is certainly his youngest daughter, Gianna Emmanuela, a geriatrician. In 2003, she left her job to devote herself entirely to her elderly father, who needed medical assistance and affection.

> *"He continued to live, until the last day, with great dignity, fortitude, serenity, and great patience, without ever complaining about his ever-greater over time physical limitations, his ever-greater difficulties in feeding himself, with the disposition of*

---

34 *Ibid.*

35 Letter posthumous from daughter Laura to her father in *Gianna Sorriso di Dio,* year 9, nos. 24–25–26, January–December 2010, p. 11.

heart to accept, as always in his life, the will of the Lord. Until the end he was a life lesson (through his example). He witnessed to the sacred good of life until his last breath, to his great love for life, to his daily thanksgiving to the Lord for all the graces he had received from Him in his long life."[36]

The Family of Origin

Pietro was born in Mesero on July 1, 1912, to Maria Salmoiraghi and Luigi Molla. "*My grandparents' families were farmers. My grandfather Luigi was a shoemaker,*" wrote the lastborn Gianna Emanuela.[37]

Luigi Molla (1884–1956) was in fact already an apprentice shoemaker at the age of eight; he then became responsible for the branch in Mesero of a shoe factory in Parabiago at the age of only twenty-one, and taught many skilled shoemakers of the surroundings. Pietro's mom, Maria (1885–1978), worked in a spinning mill and was an extremely simple woman; she married in 1907 and had the sorrow of seeing her first three sons die at a very tender age. Pietro was the first to survive, then followed by his four sisters: Maria Rosa (called Rosetta), Adelaide, Luigia, and Teresina.

Biography

His father poured his hopes mainly on Pietro, encouraging him in his studies and making him pass the fifth-grade exam (prepared by the superior of the Most Precious Blood Sisters—called Preziosine—in Mesero, Mother Giovanna Calloni) at the Canossian Sisters Institute in Magenta, since in his village the school ended at fourth grade. He then attended (the five classes of gymnasium) at the Villoresi San

---

36 From the testimony of his daughter Gianna Emanuela in *Gianna Sorriso di Dio,* year 9, nos. 24–25–26, January–December 2010, p. 17.

37 From the testimony of his daughter Gianna Emanuela in *Gianna Sorriso di Dio,* year 10, nos. 27–28–29, January–December 2011, p. 17.

Giuseppe Collegio in Monza, run by the Barnabite Fathers, a place of severe discipline and respect towards neighbor.

Later, he enrolled in the Zucchi Classical High School in Monza. These classical studies would remain among Pietro's interests, particularly his taste for refined and poetic writing, which is reflected in his letters.

Molla chose to enroll in the Faculty of Engineering at the Polytechnic University in Milan.

> *"Probably the thing I remember with more joy are the afternoons spent together in our garden in Courmayeur when I was little; he took pictures with his old camera and I, surprised by that object from past times, listened to him with curiosity while he explained to me how it worked. One of the things I remember best about him is his infinite patience in explaining to me how things worked; I think this was related to his being an engineer."*[38]

Growing esteem for him matured in the area where he lived, and his great spirit of service led him to accept, without pay, the positions proposed to him: as head of the local Fascist group, he settled the distribution of government aid in food to the families according to their needs, putting an end to the irregularities; moreover, every Sunday afternoon he taught [Catholic] doctrine to adults. In 1936, he took a degree, passed the State Exam to exercise the profession, and was called by the S.A.F.F.A. company (*Società per Azioni Fabbriche Fiammiferi ed Affini*—Joint Stock Company of Matches and Similar Goods Factories), from its main factory in Ponte Nuovo of Magenta.

Hired as technical secretary to the director, after only two years he already becomes deputy director of the Ponte Nuovo factory and responsible for plants and machinery of the other seven matches factories in Italy; all this thanks to his enormous dedication to work

---

[38] From the testimony of his niece Ortensia (Pierluigi's daughter) in *Gianna Sorriso di Dio,* year 9, nos. 24–25–26, January–December 2010, p. 19.

Pietro with his father, Luigi Molla, Mesero, 1924.

Luigi Molla and Maria Salmoiraghi with their daughters: Sister Luigia, Adelaide with Gianfranco, her son, Rosetta and Teresina, Ponte Nuovo of Magenta, Winter 1949.

Pietro (in the fourth row, second from the right) at the Villoresi San Giuseppe Collegio, Monza, 1928.

with a remarkable interest in the new technologies. His daughter, Gianna Emanuela attests:

> *"Dad, who arrived at S.A.F.F.A. very young, only 24 years old, fresh from his degree in Mechanical Industrial Engineering, found a situation of great physical fatigue for the workers and female workers employed in the matches production, and he immediately worried about them and their health. Thus, to relieve them of this fatigue, as responsible for the design and construction of new plants and new machinery for matches, he implemented the mechanizations of match production, in particular of cerini, familiari, minerva, and Swedish types.*

> *Following the reduction of manpower that the technological introduction and innovation entailed, he then worried about diversifying S.A.F.F.A.'s production to create new jobs, with great intelligence, clairvoyance and foresight, as well as love and dedication to his neighbor.*
>
> *I remember that Dad himself told me many times that he worked very much, much more than the hours he was required to work and for which he was paid, and that throughout his life he has always tried to create new jobs."*[39]

In fact, Pietro himself said:

> *"I have worked a lot, this is true, I have tried all my life to create jobs. This has been my life."*[40]

His membership in the Catholic Action (Association) saved him from implications with Fascism; when the (Second World) War broke out, he received several registered letters for cancellation of his political tasks.

On 7 March 1944 he was arrested with three workers by two Fascist soldiers of the Muti Squad; threatened with shooting, while they were about to be transferred from Magenta and handed over to the Germans, Napoleone Umberto Parmigiani, the head of the local Fascist group, ran up and arduously obtained their release, putting his own life at risk. Parmigiani, who knew Pietro for the work he had done in Mesero, intervened a second time after some months when Pietro and the director of S.A.F.F.A., Francesco Bordone, were already on a little truck headed to the concentration camps.

The S.A.F.F.A. company was (and still is) located near the Ticino bridge on the border with Piemonte; two days after the liberation

---

[39] From the testimony of his daughter Gianna Emanuela in *Gianna Sorriso di Dio,* year 10, nos. 27–28–29, January–December 2011, p. 23.

[40] P. Molla - E. Guerriero, *Gianna la donna forte. La beata Gianna Beretta Molla nel ricordo del marito,* Ed. San Paolo, Cinisello Balsamo (Milan) 1995, p. 26.

of Milan, the German anti-aircraft battery was still nearby with the American tanks aiming at it.

To protect the workers, the civilian population, and the factory, deputy director Molla mediated personally, with the help of his collaborator Giuseppe Megler, who spoke English and German very well; he invited the heads of the two departments to his office and made the driver available to allow the German officer to go to Como to ask his commander for authorization to surrender. The outcome was positive.

Molla continued his work activity by traveling a lot in Europe and around the world.

He had a brilliant working career, thanks to his skills as an engineer and company executive: in 1950, he became central director of the Ponte Nuovo factory; in 1961, he was appointed deputy general director of S.A.F.F.A.; five years later he was promoted to general director with specific responsibilities in the technical sector of this same company that then employed almost 3,500 workers.

> *"I remember, since I was a child, the great humanity of Dad, his great humility, and his deep respect for all those who worked with him: from the worker who carried out the most modest work, to the highest executive, to his superiors. I remember well that he always took off his hat in front of each of them, without distinction, in a gesture of greeting and as a sign of respect, when we happened to meet them on the street, on the ways of S.A.F.F.A. factory or of the small village of Ponte Nuovo."*[41]

On July 31, 1979, he left the position of general director to retire.

> *"He lived with pride the 'Saffa' as his second home, a workshop for building men and machines, so much so that the company with his leadership became one of the two world leaders for*

[41] From the testimony of his daughter Gianna Emanuela in *Gianna Sorriso di Dio,* year 10, nos. 27–28–29, January–December, p. 23.

matches production. A man of clear intelligence and great culture, with a soul open to his neighbor, a man who in every situation showed his great qualities such as sobriety, discretion, and humility, without ever taking advantage of any privilege. The precision was a duty, and he passed on to all his collaborators the will and the enthusiasm in always doing something new, committing all their strengths and their abilities to new goals, always supported by trust in his neighbor. He always placed his family first."[42]

Pietro was a member of the Board of Directors of S.A.F.F.A. from 1972 to 1988; he was also a member of the Executive Committee of S.A.F.F.A. from 1978 to 1986 and Advisor of both ITALMATCH in Milan and ISFA (*Industria Siciliana Fiammiferi Affini*) in Catania. From 1937 to 1978, as responsible for the design and construction of new plants and machinery for matches, he implemented the mechanizations of the productions of the types of matches than can be lit anywhere (*cerini* and *familiari*) and of the safety types (minerva and Swedish); he planned fundamental machines to produce wax and wood matches, some of which have obtained the patent in dozens of countries around the world. From 1986 to 1998 he was president of SEATEK S.p.A. (Advanced Marine Propulsion Technology) in Annone Brianza (Lecco); this company began as a factory producing turbo diesel engines for boats used for Offshore races and, subsequently, for the vehicles used in many military and paramilitary corps. From December 1956 to May 1961 he was also a member of the Board of Directors of the Hospital of Magenta.

Back in the 1950s, Pietro, focused on work, seemed to have no time for affections; but the Lord had a plan for him too.

---

[42] From the testimony by Dr. Pacifico Portaluppi, Pietro Molla's collaborator at S.A.F.F.A., in *Gianna Sorriso di Dio,* year 10, nos. 27–28–29, January–December 2011, p. 27.

Gianna and Pietro, engaged, on the slope of the Livrio, Valtellina, Sondrio, Summer 1955.

3
ENGAGEMENT

"I remember that I met Gianna, the first time in my life, in September 1949, in Magenta, in the medical office of her brother Dr. Ferdinando, to whom I had turned for an indisposition. We just looked at each other and greeted. My first impression of Gianna was of an extremely transparent and serious person. I saw her again, a second time, on April 16, 1950, in the hospital of Magenta, again in a white coat, when she had just finished a blood transfusion for my sister Teresina, whom the Lord called among His Angels a few days later. Also in that circumstance, for me extremely painful, our looks have just met."[43]

GIANNA and Pietro's first encounters are fleeting; the rumors and positive opinions about that young doctor also reach the engineer.

"Not a discordant voice among the many people I approached, but only unanimous appreciation of the limpid, exemplary witness of faith and Christian life of Gianna and her family."[44]

Gianna's work brings her closer, geographically, to Pietro.

---

[43] From Pietro's testimony in *Gianna Sorriso di Dio,* year 4, nos. 10–11, May–December 2005, p. 7.

[44] *Ibid.*

"I met her again in the Summer of 1950, when she opened her medical office in Mesero, in the house in front of mine, and chose as her nurse Mrs. Luigina Garavaglia, who lived in the same house as me. From the second half of 1950 to November 1954 there were some of our fleeting meetings, quick exchanges of greetings, and a few slight smiles, on the occasion of her visits to the nurse or her travels from Magenta to Mesero, and mine from Mesero to Magenta."[45]

Finally, they officially met when both were invited to the first Mass of Father Lino Garavaglia of Mesero (future Bishop of Cesena-Sarsina).

"In my diary of that day I remember her as with her gentle, wide, and good smile she congratulated Father Lino and his relatives; I remember her as she made, devotedly, the sign of the Holy Cross before lunch. I remember her still in prayer at the Eucharistic benediction. I still feel her cordial handshake and see again her sweet and bright smile that accompanied it. And in my diary of the following day, December 9, I wrote: 'I feel the serene tranquility that gives me the certainty that I have had the good meeting. Mary Immaculate has blessed me.'"[46]

The two young people begin dating each other; the initial shyness disappears and between Gianna and Pietro grows the knowledge and the certainty of sharing the same desires and ideals matured within deeply Christian families.

"On the evening of December 31, 1954, I attend a ballet performance with Gianna and her family at the Teatro della Scala in Milan and welcome the new year in her home. I read in my diary of that day: 'This evening can be a decisive date for my

---

45 *Ibid.*

46 *Ibid.*

life and my aspirations. I entrust myself to Our Lady of Good Counsel and to Teresina.'"[47]

Since February 1955, Gianna and Pietro intensify the occasions for meeting. Pietro recalls:

"[. . .] we confide to each other our desires and aspirations, hopes and certainties, and we understand each other better and better."[48]

Gianna is a beautiful woman, affable and spontaneous, full of a contagious enthusiasm for life, that soon causes Pietro, who is reserved and more rigid, and grew up quickly amid responsibilities, to fall in love.

"Talking with Gianna I immediately had the confirmation of my first impression; I was in front of an extremely clear, extremely charming person. It was her gaze, her attitude, her eyes, her beauty that made her so attractive. I realized that woman was good for me. I would have liked to be together with her. I had, therefore, fallen in love, but I was not able to find the words to express my feelings. Gianna, thank God, was more expansive than me, more open. I, on the other hand, had a somewhat reserved character, induced by my formation and life."[49]

Pietro, in fact, while studying at the Zucchi High School in Monza, was prefect at the Collegio San Giuseppe, that is, responsible for the discipline of a group of younger boys to be able to pay his expenses of the Collegio, where he had remained as a boarder. His brilliant working career had also begun in the name of responsibilities in the S.A.F.F.A. company, which had thousands of workers.

---

[47] *Ibid.*, pp. 7–8.

[48] *Ibid.*

[49] P. Molla - E. Guerriero, *Gianna la donna forte. La beata Gianna Beretta Molla nel ricordo del marito,* Ed. San Paolo, Cinisello Balsamo (Milan) 1995, p. 42.

Right from the start, therefore, the character complementarity of the two young people is evident.

> *"[. . .] In the very moment in which she invited me to the manifestations of liturgy and piety, she proposed to me a new model of humanity. As soon as we were engaged, I had to confess to her that I worked too much: every day until late, including Saturday and many times even on Sunday. She immediately told me: 'That's not right; it's nice to work, but it is necessary also to recreate ourselves. Look how beautiful the concerts are, let's subscribe to the concerts. The theater is also very beautiful.' And we subscribed to concerts and to the theater. She therefore taught me to live better."*[50]

On March 22, Gianna visited Pietro's house for the first time, meeting his parents and sisters.

On April 11, the official engagement is celebrated with a special Mass officiated by Gianna's brother, Don Giuseppe, in the church of the Canossian Sisters in Magenta.

> *"In the radiant summer of our engagement, Gianna was for me, more and more every day, the wonderful creature that transmitted to me her joy of living, of climbing the peaks and descending quickly from the snowy slopes, the joy of the enchantment of Creation and her ineffable smile, the joy of our new family which was now at hand, and the joy of God's grace."*[51]

Gianna was happy to realize in herself the same vocation that she had often spoken about to the young women of Catholic Action, aware that love is first of all a gift that starts from the capacity to improve your inner life:

---

50 *Ibid.,* p. 46.

51 From Pietro's testimony in *Gianna Sorriso di Dio,* year 4, nos. 10–11, May–December 2005, p. 8.

> *"You have to prepare yourself for your family right now. You can't get into this path if you don't know how to love. To love means the desire to perfect yourself, your loved one, to overcome your selfishness, to give yourself..."*[52]

As their wedding day drew nearer, Gianna proposed to Pietro that they prepare themselves with a Triduum of Holy Masses and Holy Communions, each at their own respective Marian Shrine (she in Magenta, he in Ponte Nuovo):

> *"I did it very willingly with her, but it would not have occurred to me to prepare ourselves with a Triduum."*[53]

---

[52] Cf. *Gianna Sorriso di Dio,* year 3, no. 6, April 2004, p. 7.

[53] P. Molla - E. Guerriero, *Gianna la donna forte. La beata Gianna Beretta Molla nel ricordo del marito,* Ed. San Paolo, Cinisello Balsamo (Milan) 1995, p. 44.

4
MARRIAGE

SAINT Gianna, in her intentions, had a very clear understanding of the meaning of marriage to be shared with Pietro:

> *"So, with the help and blessing of God we will do everything so that our new family can be a small cenacle where Jesus reigns over all our affections, desires, actions. [. . .] We become God's collaborators in His creation, so we can give Him children who love Him and serve Him."*[54]

These expressions are interpreted as follows by Gianna's brother, Fr. Giuseppe Beretta:

> *"In other words, you wanted to tell him that it was always living in God's grace that you proposed to live your married life with him, living matrimonial love always according to God's plan: grow, multiply and fill the earth!"*[55]

Gianna therefore lays the foundations for building her marital relationship and her new family "on the rock of the Gospel."

The long-awaited wedding day took place on a beautiful day at the end of September:

---

[54] Letter of 13 September 1955, in Gianna Beretta. Pietro Molla, *Lettere*, edited by E. Guerriero, Ed. San Paolo, Cinisello Balsamo (Milan) 2012, p. 101.

[55] From the testimony of Fr. Giuseppe Beretta in *Gianna Sorriso di Dio,* year 3, no. 7, August 2004, p. 10.

> *"Of that morning of Saturday, September 24, 1955, I still feel today the unspeakable emotion that overcame me at the sudden din of clapping, throughout the Basilica of San Martino in Magenta, at the moment in which my most beloved Gianna entered the Church, accompanied by her elder brother Francesco, until her arrival at the altar of our Wedding."*[56]

These are the words with which, fifty years later, on the occasion of the celebration of their golden wedding anniversary, Pietro recalls his wedding day with emotion. His daughter Laura emphasized:

> *"It was certainly not customary, at that time, to interfere with the solemn austerity of the rite, but that clapping, which aroused a shiver in dad, was the cordial recognition to my mom, on the part of so many people who had known her, of a life well spent, as a young woman, as a Christian committed to the apostolate and in charity, as a doctor."*[57]

Gianna and Pietro were married in a church expressly chosen by the saint for the emotional bond that had arisen there. Her husband recalls:

> *"Because of my shy and reserved character, I would have preferred to get married in a secluded small Church in the mountains, with only a few people present. I gladly made the sacrifice, a really strong one, to get married in this great Basilica so as to please my Gianna, who wanted so much to get married in her Parish, where she was at home, where even today you can feel*

---

[56] From Pietro's testimony in *Gianna Sorriso di Dio,* year 4, nos. 10–11, May–December 2005, p. 1.

[57] From the testimony of Laura Molla and her husband Giuseppe Pannuti on Saturday 17 May 2008 at the Diocesan Encounter for the Engaged at the Family Diocesan Shrine "Saint Gianna Beretta Molla" in Mesero.

her presence, breathe her air, her great faith and her great spirit of prayer."[58]

The marriage was celebrated by Gianna's brother, Fr. Giuseppe Beretta, who, as Pietro recalls, prophetically called the new couple to sanctity:

"[. . .] He affectionately exhorted us to witness to the Gospel and to holiness, following the wonderful example of their 'holy parents.'"[59]

It should be emphasized that, during the marriage, the marital home was not just any house but a little villa within the S.A.F.F.A., the company in Ponte Nuovo of Magenta where Pietro worked. The contact with the working environment, with all its problems, directly involved also the spouses:

"Then I remember the difficulties of coming to live in a small house in the enclosure of the factory that I managed: a beautiful house, but it was still in the factory. In addition, when during the three-year period 1956-58 there were rather heavy strikes, with demonstrations that were heard from our house, and I was, or I went, among the workers, Gianna faced these difficulties without ever complaining."[60]

And again, in this regard:

"And when, during the three-year period 1956-1957-1958, prolonged and very heavy strikes made her to share in direct my worries and bitternesses, she never asked me to move house; she

58 From Pietro's testimony in *Gianna Sorriso di Dio,* year 4, nos. 10–11, May–December 2005, p. 2.

59 *Ibid.*

60 P. Molla - E. Guerriero, *Gianna la donna forte. La beata Gianna Beretta Molla nel ricordo del marito,* Ed. San Paolo, Cinisello Balsamo (Milan) 1995, p. 66.

knew that this residence facilitated the fulfilment of my duties and responsibilities."[61]

Fidelity to the sacrament of marriage remained even after death: to the question "*Have you ever thought of remarrying?*" Pietro Molla answered with determination and serenity: "*No. Sincerely. We loved each other too much, and Gianna was for me an incomparable spouse and mother."*[62]

For Gianna and Pietro, the marriage formula goes beyond *"Until death do us part,"* and culminates with *"Until death makes us meet again."*

---

[61] From Pietro Molla's preface to the book Gianna Beretta Molla, *Il tuo grande amore mi aiuterà a essere forte. Lettere al marito,* edited by E. Guerriero, Ed. San Paolo, Cinisello Balsamo (Milan) 1999, p. 11.

[62] P. Molla - E. Guerriero, *Gianna la donna forte. La beata Gianna Beretta Molla nel ricordo del marito,* Ed. San Paolo, Cinisello Balsamo (Milan) 1995, p. 72.

Gianna and Pietro married, Basilica of Saint Martin, Magenta, September 24th, 1955.

5

PARENTHOOD

AMONG Dr. Beretta's intentions, there was the intention that she and Pietro would become, as spouses, "*God's collaborators in His creation*" to "*give Him children who love Him and serve Him*"; in her daily profession, Gianna often took care of children and showed a particular fondness for them.

Pietro validates this in his interviews:

> *"I had confirmation of this from the enthusiasm and joy with which she welcomed, immediately after our wedding, her appointment as health director of the Crêche of Ponte Nuovo of Magenta and as school doctor of the Nursery School and the Elementary School, also of Ponte Nuovo. [. . .] On the other hand, Gianna had already been a delegate of the Very Little Girls' Section of Catholic Action during her high school years."*[63]

This great love for little children naturally led her to desire to have a large family herself, aware that life is a gift from God, the most beautiful gift, and that children are neither a burden nor obstacle to self-fulfillment, but rather a blessing.

On their desire to give life because they were in love with life, Pietro himself testifies:

> *"Gianna and I wanted to have more than one child. We loved life and wanted others to have it."*[64]

---

63 *Ibid.*, p. 67.

64 *Ibid.*, p. 47.

The responsibility of being parents, however, was never underestimated by the Molla spouses, as Pietro testifies:

> *"We had also prepared ourselves with a certain awe to welcoming children, asking ourselves the question that belongs to everyone: 'Will we be able to raise them well?' Then we had another little worry. After the birth of our first child, we asked ourselves: 'If we have other children, how are we going to love them like this one?'"*[65]

Gianna, in her first months of marriage, is impatient and wants nothing other than children; in fact, she writes, confiding in her, to her sister, Mother Virginia:

> *"Unfortunately, I still don't feel the symptoms of pregnancy. Pray that the Lord will soon send me many good and healthy children."*[66]

Five months after their wedding, her first pregnancy was announced. On November 19, 1956, Pierluigi was born at their Ponte Nuovo home.

Gianna's pregnancies were not so simple; the desire to give life to new creatures and to comply with the will of God was so strong that it overcame the ailments and the indispositions, putting aside the selfishness that leads to the search only for one's own well-being. Her husband himself testifies to this:

> *"During each pregnancy Gianna suffered a lot. And how much she really suffered I learned only after her death, because she carefully hid it from me. I knew of vomiting and heartburn, but not of other sufferings."*[67]

---

65 *Ibid.*

66 G. Pelucchi, *L'amore più grande. Santa Gianna Beretta Molla.* Ed. Paoline, Milan 2004, p. 107.

67 P. Molla - E. Guerriero, *Gianna la donna forte. La beata Gianna Beretta Molla nel ricordo del marito,* Ed. San Paolo, Cinisello Balsamo (Milan) 1995, p. 66.

On December 11, 1957, Maria Zita, called by everyone Mariolina, was born at the Ponte Nuovo home.

Laura was born in the same house on July 15, 1959. The family trend continues with enthusiasm and constant reliance on Our Lady:

> *"You desired, as soon as the ceremony of Holy Baptism was over, that each of our children be consecrated and entrusted to the particular protection of Our Lady of Good Counsel and that I would read the prayer of consecration myself."*[68]

Obviously, there was no lack of daily problems and difficulties, which also emerge from the uninterrupted correspondence between Gianna and Pietro: the distance of her husband while traveling and the concerns for the health of the children.

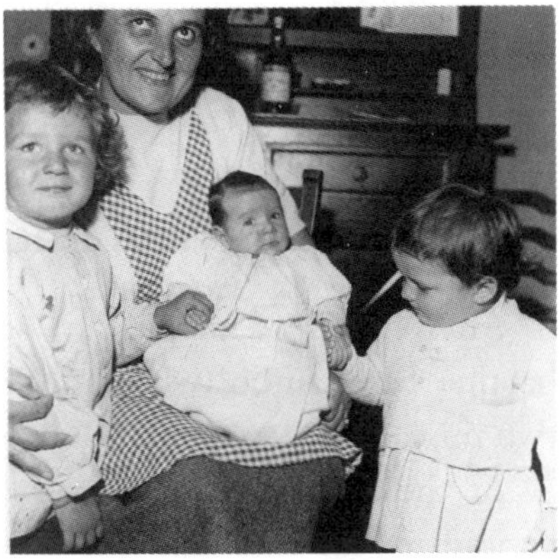

Pietro with Mariolina and Pierluigi on the steps of the Shrine of Notre Dame de la Guérison, Val Veny, Courmayeur, Aosta, Summer 1958.

Gianna with Laura, Mariolina, and Pierluigi, Courmayeur, Aosta, August 1959.

The spouses agree on a specific model of education through which to raise their children; the "education through persuasion" has been inherited from their families of origin, and is intended to be passed down to the new generations:

---

68 Pietro Molla, *Fidanzata, sposa e madre*, in *Terra Ambrosiana*, year XXXXV, no. 1, January–February 1994, p. 41.

"The model of education that Gianna had proposed to me was the same model in which she had grown up: the education through persuasion. She told me: 'I do not conceive of the mother giving a slap to her child. We must succeed in educating them with persuasion and above all educating them, from the very earliest years, to see in everything a gift of God and to have respect for this gift.' When Gianna proposed this educational model, she found me perfectly in agreement. In fact, I too have had the fortune of having parents who have educated me through persuasion."[69]

Gianna's educational ideal was the one she received in her family of origin:

"I don't remember them ever laying their hands on us. My father and my mother convinced us with reasoning. They were strict . . . but they never beat us."[70]

"Choose—and I demand it—the baby!"

After her third pregnancy, according to the testimony of her brother Ferdinando (who monitored her as a doctor), Gianna had two miscarriages, of which the cause could not be determined.[71]

At the end of the Summer of 1961, a new motherhood was announced for Gianna:

"You longed so much for another child, you prayed, and you asked people to pray that the Lord would hear you. The Lord

---

[69] P. Molla - E. Guerriero, *Gianna la donna forte. La beata Gianna Beretta Molla nel ricordo del marito,* Ed. San Paolo, Cinisello Balsamo (Milan) 1995, p. 65.

[70] From the testimony of her brother, Fr. Giuseppe Beretta, in G. Pelucchi, *L'amore più grande. Santa Gianna Beretta Molla,* Ed. Paoline, Milan 2004, p. 28.

[71] Cf. Gianna Beretta. Pietro Molla, *Lettere*, edited by E. Guerriero, Ed. San Paolo, Cinisello Balsamo (Milan) 2012, p. 42, note 28 and p. 23, note 4.

heard you, but this divine grace would ask you for the offering of your life. And you did it."[72]

The events of the last months of Gianna's life are retraced by the words of Pietro, who addresses his wife directly:

> "*In September 1961, forced to undergo surgery for voluminous fibromyoma in the uterus during the new pregnancy, you asked, without hesitation, that the surgeon be primarily concerned to save the life of your little creature, saving the pregnancy. It was your full trust in Providence and the certainty in the decisive efficacy of prayer that gave you the courage for that decision.*"[73]

Gianna Emanuela, the daughter who would be born, recalls:

> "*When I grew up and was able to understand my Mom's extreme sacrifice which crowned her exemplary Christian life, it was my Dad who explained to me the reason for her choice, thus helping me to overcome the feelings of guilt I had concerning my siblings, from childhood, and to cheer me up. The fundamental choice Mom made at the end of the second month of her pregnancy with me, as my uncle Fr. Giuseppe also always tells me, when a voluminous fibromyoma, a benign tumor, appeared in her uterus. As Dad testified in April 1973, in the book he dedicated to my siblings and me, Mom was free in that worrisome situation to choose and decide between three solutions:*
>
> *—The first: remove the fibroid, terminate that pregnancy, and exclude the possibility of having other pregnancies (the safest and the least risky solution for her life in that pregnancy and for the future)*
>
> *—the second: remove the fibroid, terminate that pregnancy, and preserve the possibility of other pregnancies (the safest and*

[72] Pietro Molla, *Fidanzata, sposa e madre*, in *Terra Ambrosiana,* year XXXXV, no. 1, January–February 1994, p. 42.
[73] *Ibid.*

> *the least risky solution for her life in that pregnancy and not for the future)*
>
> *—the third: remove the fibroid, do not terminate that pregnancy, and preserve the possibility of other pregnancies (the riskiest and the most worrying solution for her life in that pregnancy and for the future).*
>
> *My Mom chose, decided, and asked the surgeon for the third solution. And before the surgery to remove the fibroma, well aware of the risk that the continuation of the pregnancy would have entailed—the risk that a suture, made on the uterus in the first months of pregnancy, could give way, causing a secondary rupture of the uterus and mortal danger to herself, as well as to the child—she begged the surgeon to save the life she was carrying in her womb, mine, and entrusted herself to prayer and to Providence. My life was saved. Mom thanked the Lord and spent the seven months leading up to childbirth with incomparable fortitude and unchanged commitment as a mother and doctor."*[74]

Gianna was a doctor: she knew her clinical situation perfectly and was aware of the risks that her choice entailed.

The satisfaction for the good outcome of the operation, performed by the head of the Monza Hospital, Professor Mario Vitali, was overshadowed by concern for the future.

> *"How much you suffered for that operation and with what joy you thanked the Lord because your motherhood was saved! And you, doctor, and pediatrician, were well aware that, in those conditions, the saved pregnancy undoubtedly put your life at serious risk. With incomparable fortitude and unchanged commitment, you continued your mission as a mother and doctor. I remember that your usual smile and your usual serenity for*

---

74 From the testimony of her daughter Gianna Emanuela in *Gianna Sorriso di Dio,* year 11, nos. 30–31–32, January–December 2012, p. 6.

> *the beauty, liveliness and health of our children were many times veiled by an intimate concern. You feared and trembled that the little creature in your womb could be born suffering. You prayed and prayed that this would not be the case. Several times you asked me for forgiveness if you were causing me worry. You told me that never as then did you need lovingness and understanding. You never spoke a word to me, in all those long months, about your awareness, as a doctor, of what awaited you. And you certainly did this so as not to make me suffer. I was worried about your silent tidying, for days and days, every corner of our house, every drawer, every dress, every personal object, as if you were going on a very long journey. When it seemed more and more probable to you that it was not possible to save you and the creature you were expecting, you never despaired of Providence, you prayed for the salvation of both, even if ready to the sacrifice of your life."*[75]

A dispute could arise: Gianna, who loves life, her husband, and her children, how could she choose to let them grow up without a mother?

Her husband Pietro replies:

> *"It was a choice that can be well understood and rightly evaluated only in the light of Gianna's firm convictions, her conscience as a mother and her unquestionable trust in Providence. Gianna was firmly convinced that the baby she was carrying in her womb was a person to be loved, to be respected and not an object on which to exercise one's will. It was certainly a dramatic choice. The more I think about it, the more I realize that it must have been a tremendous sacrifice for this woman. After all, it was a cruel dilemma: either sacrifice the child or give one's life with the consequence of leaving four children without*

---

[75] Pietro Molla, *Fidanzata, sposa e madre*, in *Terra Ambrosiana*, year XXXXV, no. 1, January–February 1994, p. 42.

a mother; a choice to which many object. I do not feel like saying anything about it except to emphasize Gianna's trust in Providence."[76]

Gianna's sister, Mother Virginia, speaks along the same lines:

"To understand it is necessary to believe, like Gianna, in Providence. My mother always said an ancient proverb: 'Every child is born with his own little bundle.' Gianna was very sure that God would provide for her children, and for that life that was now coming, which she carried in her womb, she had all her respect. Gianna trusted in Providence."[77]

Her husband continues, addressing his wife directly:

"You knew that the maternal contribution in raising, educating and forming our children has no equal, but in your humility and above all in the fullness of your trust in Providence, you were persuaded not to do an act of injustice to our three children, because in that painful circumstance the one who needed you primarily and indispensably was the creature in your womb, and while considering your duty to raise, educate and form our children no less seriously than the duty to ensure bringing them into the world after conception, you relied fully on Providence for their education and formation if this new maternity would have required the sacrifice of your life."[78]

Entrustment to God's will, the trust in Providence—in a word, faith—characterized this mother faced with such a painful situation.

---

76 P. Molla - E. Guerriero, *Gianna la donna forte. La beata Gianna Beretta Molla nel ricordo del marito,* Ed. San Paolo, Cinisello Balsamo (Milan) 1995, p. 68.

77 G. Pelucchi, *L'amore più grande. Santa Gianna Beretta Molla,* Ed. Paoline, Milan 2004, p. 33.

78 Pietro Molla, *Fidanzata, sposa e madre,* in *Terra Ambrosiana,* year XXXXV, no. 1, January–February 1994, p. 42.

A decision that, of course, also involves the husband and father of the creature:

> *"My Dad, who knew very well the generosity of my Mom, her spirit of sacrifice, the thoughtfulness and strength of her choices and decisions, felt himself in the obligation of conscience to have to respect them, even if they could have extremely painful consequences for him and my siblings. So, if I was able to come into the world, it is also thanks to him, who did not oppose it, but respected the choice and the decision of my Mom to put my life before hers, if a decision had to be made between her and me. Mom's choice, Dad told me, a choice made against the tide, was dictated by her conscience as a mother and doctor and can be well understood only in the light of her faith, of her firm conviction of the sacred right to life, of the heroism of maternal love and of full trust in Providence."*[79]

A few days before giving birth, Gianna told Pietro "*in a firm and at the same time serene tone of voice*" to save the baby's life if it was necessary to choose.

> *"On the morning of Holy Saturday, April 21, 1962, we had the ineffable joy and the divine gift of the creature we were waiting for: Gianna Emanuela. After a few hours, your unheard-of sufferings began, sufferings that were beyond your strength and that made you call out to your mother at every moment, who was already in Paradise. You knew you were going to die, and you felt the torment of leaving all our children still very young, but you did not confide it to me. When you took our little creature in your arms, you looked at her very, very lovingly, with a look that betrayed your indescribable suffering of not being able to enjoy her, to raise her, and to never see her again [. . .].*

---

79 From the testimony of his daughter Gianna Emanuela in *Gianna Sorriso di Dio,* year 11, nos. 30–31–32, January–December 2012, p. 6.

> *I remember what you said to me on Wednesday morning, with a serenity so very sweet that it seemed to me almost otherworldly: 'Pietro, now I am healed. Pietro, I was already beyond and if you knew what I have seen. One day I will tell you. But because we were too happy, we were too well, with our wonderful children, full of health and grace, with all the blessings of Heaven, they sent me back here below to suffer again, because it is not right to present ourselves to the Lord without many sufferings.' This was and remains for me your testament of joy and suffering."*[80]

Gianna, in her agony, prays constantly and asks to receive the Eucharist; at dawn on Saturday, April 28, Pietro obtains permission from the doctors to bring Gianna, now in extreme agony, back to her marital home in Ponte Nuovo of Magenta.

> *"Maybe you too heard the voices of our children who were waking up in the next room. Almost at the same time you entered Paradise."*[81]

Gianna dies in her bed at eight o'clock in the morning. Gianna had given everything, even her life, to honor her role as life-bearer; now the role of parent and educator was Pietro's alone. It was indispensable to think of the small children, and of the newborn:

> *"When Gianna passed away, I had to react a great deal so as not to be overwhelmed by the weight of responsibility and by the duties I had towards our children, who were orphaned at such a tender age. I prayed so much to Gianna to watch over us, to protect us, to help us. I experienced that she watched over us and greatly helped us. Gianna's relatives and mine were so very generous and helpful. The newborn baby girl was the object of particularly*

---

[80] Pietro Molla, *Fidanzata, sposa e madre*, in *Terra Ambrosiana,* year XXXXV, no. 1, January–February 1994, pp. 42-43.

[81] *Ibid.*, p. 43.

Pietro with Mariolina and Pierluigi at the ceremony of the Blessing of the bells of the new Church dedicated to Saint Joseph the Worker, Ponte Nuovo of Magenta, 1963.

affectionate care. Thanks be to God, my children grew up well honoring the memory and witness of their mother."[82]

As Pietro himself recalls, it is the children, with their simple and sure faith, who gave him the first input of trust and hope:

> *"How many times do they come back to my mind the four questions that Pierluigi, our dearest firstborn—he was not yet five and a half years old—addressed to me as we left the small Church of Ponte Nuovo after the Holy Mass of your funeral. He then asked me, with a crescendo that made me sob: 'Does Mommy still see me? . . . Does Mommy still hear me? . . . Does Mommy still touch me? . . . Does Mommy still think about me? . . .' My answers were four 'Yeses' dictated by faith and trust in Jesus."*[83]

---

[82] P. Molla - E. Guerriero, *Gianna la donna forte. La beata Gianna Beretta Molla nel ricordo del marito,* Ed. San Paolo, Cinisello Balsamo (Milan) 1995, p. 72.

[83] Pietro Molla, *Fidanzata, sposa e madre,* in *Terra Ambrosiana,* year XXXXV, no. 1, January–February 1994, p. 43.

Gianna's funeral was celebrated on the afternoon of April 30, 1962, in the small Church of Our Lady of Good Counsel in Ponte Nuovo of Magenta; the ceremony was a great unanimous manifestation of deep emotion, faith, and prayer. Above the door of the church, a banner stood out with these words:

> *"Deeply moved, we remember Dr. Gianna Molla, née Beretta, who consciously offered herself for the life of her daughter Gianna Emanuela."*

There were many reactions of esteem and admiration for Gianna, who in the final gesture of offering her life for the birth of her baby girl had crowned an exemplary life of joyful faith and fraternal charity. Gianna's testimony straightaway caused an "immediate effect" in the simple faith of her people:

> *"But, perhaps, the most significant thing was what the parish priest of Ponte Nuovo, Fr. Agostino Cerri, confided: he said he had never seen as many Easter Communions as that year, of men above all, who felt the need—or the duty—to go to Confession before going to pay homage to her body or to participate worthily in the funeral."*[84]

Gianna was temporarily buried in the Chapel of the Parish Priests in the Cemetery of Mesero, Pietro's birthplace, until her remains were transferred, in 1965, to the Molla family Chapel, located in the same cemetery.

The Death of a Child

Now a widower supported by relatives, Daddy Pietro engaged in the daily process of educating and raising his four children.

---

[84] E. Apeciti, *Gianna Beretta Molla. Amare la vita,* Centro Ambrosiano, Milan 2004, pp. 65–66.

But the mystery of pain touched this man's life again, with the greatest pain a father can feel.

At the beginning of 1964, his second-born daughter Maria Zita, called Mariolina, contracted acute glomerulonephritis and was hospitalized at the hospital of Imperia, where she attended the boarding school *Sorriso d'Italia* directed by Sister Luigia Molla (Pietro's sister). She was then transferred to the Niguarda Hospital in Milan, where she died.

> *"She affectionately addressed her last words to me: 'Go back home, daddy, you're tired.' After a few hours, she died reciting the Hail Mary. 'Blessed is Mariolina who is in Paradise with Mom' were the first words of Pierluigi and Laura upon their arrival from Imperia, and their certainty restrained my weeping and made me recall Jesus urging us that, unless we become as little children, we shall not enter the Kingdom of Heaven."*[85]

Daddy Pietro, comforted by the innocence of his children, must still bear the weight of the cross with great fortitude, without letting himself be crushed, to keep his family moving forward serenely.

> *"After two very sorrowful bereavements within two years, my mother in 1962 and only two years later in 1964 my sister Mariolina, dad found himself to be the guide and support to my growth and that of my sisters, trying, if possible, to alleviate the suffering of growing up without the mother figure. He succeeded in doing this very well, thanks to his great love, to the care and sensibility with which he has always accompanied us and supported us, and to his advice, which was never imposed but always available."*[86]

---

85 Pietro Molla, *Fidanzata, sposa e madre*, in *Terra Ambrosiana*, year XXXXV, no. 1, January–February 1994, p. 43.

86 From the testimony of his son Pierluigi in *Gianna Sorriso di Dio*, year 9, nos. 24–25–26, January–December 2010, p. 10.

Humanly and spiritually put to the test, Pietro Molla faced all these sufferings with the help of an unshakeable faith in God and in His providential designs:

> *"I confess that I have long sought an explanation for the fact that the Lord did not accept my pleas, those of family members and of very many other people, so that Gianna's life was saved together with that of the baby girl she had delivered. [. . .] I had to persuade myself that pain remains a mystery even in the light of our faith, and I experienced in myself that the only way to accept it, is that of Jesus Crucified."*[87]

---

87 P. Molla - E. Guerriero, *Gianna la donna forte. La beata Gianna Beretta Molla nel ricordo del marito,* Ed. San Paolo, Cinisello Balsamo (Milan) 1995, p. 71.

6
GIANNA AND PIETRO'S MARITAL JOURNEY THROUGH THEIR CORRESPONDENCE

NOWADAYS, writing letters is no longer common. Swept away by the immediacy of the internet and by interconnectivity, today's society has lost the pleasure of exchanging letters, especially love letters.

In the 1950s, it was still customary to correspond through letters. Gianna and Pietro have left us, as precious testimony, their simple and extraordinary love letters: simple in their language, tone, and everyday nature of the topics (from the list of utensils to take on vacation to worries about a toothache); extraordinary for the level of spousal spirituality that they are able to radiate, an indelible witness of a married life founded on the authentically Christian values and principles, of a family life desired as a "*cenacle*" and *domestic church* according to the teachings of the Gospel. Cardinal Carlo Maria Martini also emphasizes the extraordinariness of these love letters, both in the frequency:

> *"A frequency that may even seem excessive, but that says more than any word how the two could not be and think of each other without communicating, without talking about themselves, their feelings, what they did, their joys and efforts, their concerns, their faith,"*[88]

and in the communication (between the two spouses).

---

[88] From Cardinal C.M. Martini's preface to the book Gianna Beretta Molla, *Il tuo grande amore mi aiuterà a essere forte. Lettere al marito,* edited by E. Guerriero, Ed. San Paolo, Cinisello Balsamo (Milan) 1999, p. 6.

Pietro and Gianna had the desire, the fervor to communicate, to relate continuously.

> *"'Communicating' first as an engaged couple and then as husband and wife—that is 'communicating within the family'—is a sign and nourishment of true love and is an expression of authentic family life. [. . .] The family is—by its nature and by its innate vocation—communication! A communication that tends to a total and reciprocal self-giving between the spouses, who feel called to forever lead a life 'as two' and 'in two.' A communication, moreover, that becomes so concrete as to make of the family both the only truly human place in which to generate and communicate new life, cooperating with God the Creator and almost interpreting His plan of love (cf.* Gaudium et Spes, *n. 50), and as the original and primary circle in which, day after day, a meaning for life is expressed, communicated, and built up, through the educational mission of the parents."*[89]

The complete correspondence of the letters between Gianna and Pietro has been published in its entirety in the volume edited by Elio Guerriero, entitled Gianna Beretta. Pietro Molla. *Lettere*. The book was published by the San Paolo Publishing House in 2012; a new edition of the work was published by Cantagalli Publishers in 2023. The editor himself writes in the introduction:

> *"In the Positio of Saint Gianna, Antonio Rimoldi accurately reports the letters, notes, and postcards written by Gianna Beretta Molla to her husband, family, friends, and other people she knew. The letters to her husband, faithfully reported here below, are 73. As far as Pietro Molla's letters are concerned, we have the very diligent archiving work which the engineer himself carried out, assisted in his last years by his daughter Gianna*

89 *Ibid.*, p. 5.

Emanuela, who also took on the arduous task of transcribing and typing his letters reported here below."[90]

Gianna Emanuela herself confirms, symbolically addressing her father:

"*And so, in agreement with Laura and Pierluigi, I started to transcribe, with all my good will and all my commitment, one by one, your 73 letters, 39 postcards, 11 notes—all written with your fountain pen and green ink—and your telegram to Mom, then comparing the transcription, word for word, and several times, with your original manuscript, which is not easy to read because of your complex handwriting, so that it was really in conformity with and faithful to your original. What a long and meticulous work it was necessary to do; I was more than pleased, honored, and deeply edified, by it.*"[91]

The complete correspondence between Saint Gianna Beretta and her husband Pietro Molla marks out the stages of a short but extremely intense marital journey because it was based on their mutual will to be a couple, an authentically Christian family, even in the trifles or in the daily difficulties.

It is Molla himself who defines, prophetically in one of his letters, this exchange of missives as an "*affectionate diary*", which he will be able to re-read to relive those moments and those feelings:

"*These, along with all the others you have written to me in my long, indeed too long absence, I will always keep close to the very sweet letters of our engagement and of my short trips abroad. Rereading them also in the future, I will relive the joy that they now bring me, I will have an affectionate diary of you and of our wonderful treasures, and they will always tell me of how*

90 Gianna Beretta. Pietro Molla, *Lettere*, edited by E. Guerriero, Ed. San Paolo, Cinisello Balsamo (Milan) 2012, p. 49.

91 *Ibid.*, from Gianna Emanuela Molla's preface to the letters of her father, p. 17.

> *much immense very sweet love you have always surrounded me with and how so gently and wisely you have been able to preserve in our treasures their thought and their longing for their far-away Dad."*[92]

This "*diary*" is a hymn to love and family; today it is available to everyone thanks to the will of Pietro Molla, who decided to consent to the publication of the entire correspondence only after his death for reasons related to the reserved nature of his character; the letters of Gianna to her husband had already been published in 1999.[93] In fact, the daughter Gianna Emanuela specifies:

> *"I remember well that you, being the very reserved person you were, always preferred to postpone this publication until after the Lord had called you to Himself, and your will was rightly respected."*[94]

Engagement

> *"One of the most touching 'relics' I keep of my wife are precisely her letters from our engagement period. [. . .] The letters in which Gianna expressed her concept of marriage, the vision she had of marriage preparation, the way she prepared for the sacrament of love, the joy she felt facing this event and the whole of life itself, are her letters from our engagement."*[95]

---

92 *Ibid.*, letter of 11 June 1959, pp. 262–263.

93 Gianna Beretta Molla, *Il tuo grande amore mi aiuterà a essere forte. Lettere al marito,* edited by E. Guerriero, Ed. San Paolo, Cinisello Balsamo (Milan) 1999.

94 From Gianna Emanuela Molla's preface to the letters of her father, in Gianna Beretta. Pietro Molla, *Lettere*, edited by E. Guerriero, Ed. San Paolo, Cinisello Balsamo (Milan) 2012, p. 16.

95 P. Molla - E. Guerriero, *Gianna la donna forte. La beata Gianna Beretta Molla nel ricordo del marito,* Ed. San Paolo, Cinisello Balsamo (Milan) 1995, p. 44.

Gianna and Pietro engaged, Sestrière, Turin, April 1955.

The correspondence of their engagement period includes fourteen letters from Pietro and eleven from Gianna; the writings were sent from January 12, 1955, about a month after their first official meeting, to September 23 of the same year, the eve of the wedding.

> *"But the discourse expands. From these letters also emerges her joy over the beauty and enchantment of creation, to which corresponded, for her part, an attitude of gratitude and thanksgiving to the Creator."*[96]

Gianna indeed loves life and nature, and from her first letters she involves Pietro with her enthusiasm, telling him of wonderful days spent skiing, days given by God amidst the wonder of creation.

> *"Yesterday and today, splendid sunny days. [. . .] It's wonderful. When you are at the very height, with a clear sky, the very white snow, how you enjoy and praise God. Pietro, you already*

96 *Ibid.*

know it, I feel so happy when I am in contact with such beautiful nature, that I would spend hours contemplating it."[97]

Language and Poetry

The first letter that Pietro writes to Gianna is sent from Stockholm (during one of his many business trips); he calls her "*Kind Doctor,*" addressing her with the formal "*Lei,*" thanking her for the pleasant time spent together (after they attended a ballet show together at the *Teatro alla Scala* in Milan for the last day of the year 1954, the two had begun dating) and telling her about his current trip.

> *"Kind Doctor,*
>
> *An unending succession of visits, meetings, and even banquets with their endless and heavy Nordic ceremonials, has allowed me to rest only a few hours a day, and I have arrived till this evening without having renewed to you the most vivid and dutiful thanks for the beautiful and pleasant evening spent together. The memory of that evening has returned to me very frequently in these days.*
>
> *My work, on my journey, has been excellent: I will complete it by Friday, and I plan to return by Sunday or Monday.*
>
> *The sky has almost always been clear, although pale in its colors from dawn to dusk; the sun is almost always out, even if it appears so distant; snow everywhere, but the cold was less than I expected; only a few degrees below zero.*
>
> *On my return, I will tell you about the 'curiosities' of my trip.*
>
> *A cordial greeting*
> *from*
> *Pietro Molla."*[98]

---

97 Letter of 23 March 1955, in Gianna Beretta. Pietro Molla, *Lettere*, edited by E. Guerriero, Ed. San Paolo, Cinisello Balsamo (Milan) 2012, pp. 73–74.

98 *Ibid.*, letter of 12 January 1955, pp. 67–68.

In her first letter, Gianna is decidedly more "direct," immediately revealing her jovial and expansive character: in fact, she begins with a "*Dearest Pietro*" and uses the informal "*tu,*" convinced that the time has come to break down the barriers of formality and move on to greater confidence.

"Dearest Pietro,

Sorry if I decisively start my writing by calling you by name and addressing you as "tu." After yesterday's meeting, in which we mutually opened up, I think we can move on to this degree of confidence that will allow us to understand each other more and more and to love each other. [. . .]

Goodbye, dear Pietro, forgive my familiarity, but that is how I am."[99]

In her first letters, Gianna expresses all her enthusiasm; although they are not teenagers (Gianna was thirty-two years old, Pietro forty-two), the language of lovers is fresh, tender, and self-aware. The style of Gianna and Pietro's letters is almost reminiscent of the biblical Canticle of Canticles, a collection of poems in which two young people express their mutual love in the alternating of different situations: the joy of encounter, the pain of separation, and the search for the beloved. In this biblical book, the feelings of a young man and a young woman are presented in poetic form with words full of sweetness and gestures of affection; the same feelings are found (in Gianna and Pietro's letters) with more modern, but still poetic tones. Pietro writes:

"Now it is night, but I have here before me your dearest image, in all its very sweet beauty, in its smile, all light and fullness of affection for me who loves you with the same immense love. [. . .] And I thank you, I thank you very, very affectionately, and I always think of you and kiss you with a long, very sweet kiss."[100]

99 *Ibid.*, letter of 21 February 1955, pp. 68–69.

100 *Ibid.*, letter of 4 September 1955, p. 89.

As in the Canticle of Canticles, both the sufferings caused by the separation of the two lovers and the intense desire to meet again are communicated.

> *"Only you are missing, Pietro, and I already look forward to the joy of having you with me on Saturday and Sunday. I will certainly come to meet you and spend the last hours of my vacation with you."*[101]

It is not difficult to find expressions of rare poetry in their early writings; it is above all Pietro who, with great gusto, dedicates to his fiancée words worthy of a poet.

His daughter, Gianna Emanuela, also confirms:

> *"[. . .] reading some of your letters with you, I said to you, with all my heart and my joy: 'Dad, but you are a poet!' and you smiled at me, and you were so pleased with my joy."*[102]

For Pietro, still in Magenta for work, to find the beauty and affection in Gianna's photographs on vacation in Sestriere is in fact a "*balm of serenity and of life:*"

> *"Looking at you, O dearest Gianna, and your sweet beauty and reading your great affection in your gaze is a balm of serenity and of life for me."*[103]

The gifts exchanged on the day of their official engagement (a ring and a watch) are an opportunity for Pietro to express metaphors of rare beauty.

> *"My jewel is you, very sweet and so gently dear in virtue and goodness, in beauty, and in your smile. My love for you always*

101 *Ibid.*, letter of 21 March 1955, pp. 72–73.

102 *Ibid.*, from Gianna Emanuela Molla's preface to the letters of her father, p. 18.

103 *Ibid.*, letter of 28 March 1955, p. 76.

wants to be more intense than the reflections of light of your ring of our engagement!

The beautiful watch you gave me accompanies me in the most beautiful time of my life: the time of our love and of our family."[104]

Even the beauty of the northern European landscapes visited by Pietro during a working trip to Sweden is a source of inspiration to express words of love to Gianna:

"Yesterday, before midnight, after I wrote you the letter, I went up again on the highest deck of the ship. The clouds had disappeared and the moon, with a slightly veiled silvery glow, was reflected in the flickering waves in the Baltic breeze. The lunar reflection appeared to me like a vivid river of infinite, soft flames: a river that, starting from my ship, reached far, far, up to you. And I felt you like this, just as close as on the moonlit evenings spent together in the peace of your garden. I have sent you another kiss, a long kiss with the wish of a night full of peace like that of the trembling waves kissed by the moon."[105]

The collection of writings from their engagement period closes with a note sent the day before their wedding, and which accompanied a watch and a pearl necklace given to Gianna from Pietro, from Pietro's mother, and, symbolically, from Gianna's deceased mother; it is another example of great poetry:

"Gianna,
So that they (these gifts) may crown the wonder
and the candor of your beauty and your virtues,
on the day of our Wedding,
and so that, one gift (the watch), may always tell
the most beautiful and serene time of our life,
and the pearls of the other (gift)

---

104 *Ibid.*, letter of 15 April 1955, p. 79.

105 *Ibid.*, letter of 6 September 1955, p. 92.

may sing the light of the enchantment of our Love,
they are given to you,
with maternal affection, your Mother and my Mother,
and with the greatest love
your Pietro."[106]

The Ideal of A Wife

Gianna and Pietro entrust their intentions to the pen, living their engagement period as a time of grace to get to know each other, share desires and fears, and prepare to lay the foundations for a serious and conscious promise. Mutual sentiments of deep respect, esteem, and support emerge from their writings.

Gianna declares from her first letter her desire to be loved, for being already orphaned by both parents, and for having found the fullness of affection in Pietro:

> *"I have not yet told you that I have always been a creature eager for affection and very sensitive. As long as I had my parents, their affection was enough for me; then, while remaining very united to the Lord and working for Him, I felt the need for a mother, and I found her in that dear nun*[107] *I told you about yesterday. Now there is you, whom I already love."*[108]

The same thing applies to Pietro who, after the age of forty years, finds in Gianna the right person with whom to form a family of his own:

> *"I had so much need and so much desire for affection and a family of my own. Now I have you, your affection and your gift, and I am happy."*[109]

---

[106] *Ibid.*, from a handwritten note of 23 September 1955, p. 102.

[107] Sister Marianna Meregalli, met at Magenta in the years 1945–1949.

[108] Letter of 21 February 1955, in Gianna Beretta. Pietro Molla, *Lettere*, edited by E. Guerriero, Ed. San Paolo, Cinisello Balsamo (Milan) 2012, pp. 68–69.

[109] *Ibid.*, letter of 22 February 1955, p. 69.

A serene and full faith emerges from Gianna's writings; at the beginning of their engagement, she is explicit and clear with Pietro:

> *"[...] I intend to give myself to form a truly Christian family."*[110]

The logic of the gift of self, without shadows of selfishness, is also deduced from Gianna's desire to be a perfect companion. It is surprising that from her first letter, Gianna, who has only recently begun to date Pietro, writes:

> *"I would really want to make you happy and be the one you desire: good, understanding and ready for the sacrifices that life will ask of us."*[111]

Her future spouse responds with the same desire to fulfil the joy of the other:

> *"My affection is for you, and with you I want to form my family. I, too, want to make you happy and fully understand you."*[112]

From what emerges since the beginning of their epistolary exchange, the love of Gianna and Pietro seems to put into practice St. Paul's exhortation: "*compete in esteeming one other.*"[113]

The doubt of not being up to the task of a wife concerns, however, even the future saint:

> *"You are the man I wanted to meet, but I do not deny that I ask myself several times: 'Will I be worthy of him?' Yes, worthy of you, Pietro, because I feel like such a nothing, so capable of nothing, that although I greatly desire to make you happy, I am afraid of not succeeding."*[114]

---

110 *Ibid.*, letter of 21 February 1955, p. 69.

111 *Ibid.*, p. 68.

112 *Ibid.*, letter of 22 February 1955, p. 69.

113 Romans 12:10.

114 Letter of 11 March 1955, in Gianna Beretta. Pietro Molla, *Lettere*, edited by E. Guerriero, Ed. San Paolo, Cinisello Balsamo (Milan) 2012, p. 70.

Moreover, Gianna identifies the holy women of the Bible as models, showing that she always draws from the Word of God, and compares herself with them:

> *"I often like to meditate on the passage from the Epistle of the Mass of St. Anne. 'Who will find a strong woman? . . . The heart of her husband can trust in her . . . she will do him only good, and she will never harm him, throughout all of his life'*[115] *etc. Pietro, may I be for you the strong woman of the Gospel!*[116] *Instead, I seem and I feel myself weak. This means that I will lean on your strong arm."*[117]

Pietro, as can always be deduced from his letters, reassures her:

> *"You are for me the strong woman of the Gospel. Near to you my joy is perfect."*[118]

Already during the period of their engagement, the will to create a stable communion between each other emerges clearly; a communion that has its source in the sacrament of the Eucharist:

> *"I love you so, so much Pietro, and you are always present to me, starting from the morning when during the Holy Mass, at the Offertory, I offer your work with mine, your joys, your sufferings, and then throughout the day until the evening."*[119]

---

[115] Beginning of the poem of praise to the virtuous woman in Proverbs 31:10–31.

[116] 'Gospel' indicates, in this case, the Holy Scripture.

[117] Letter of 9 April 1955, in Gianna Beretta. Pietro Molla, *Lettere*, edited by E. Guerriero, Ed. San Paolo, Cinisello Balsamo (Milan) 2012, pp. 77–78.

[118] *Ibid.*, letter of 15 April 1955, p. 79.

[119] *Ibid.*, letter of 10 June 1955, p. 83.

Fears

In addition to the concern of not being a spouse worthy of Pietro, Gianna also harbors the most common fears, which are less spiritual and more concrete: the fear of not pleasing her future parents-in-law and future sisters-in-law.

> *"Dear Pietro, when your mother told us last Sunday that if she should see you unhappy later on, she doesn't know what she would do, the doubt dawned on me that I was not suitable for you, that is, not good and understanding enough."*[120]

This is a sign of great humanity and humility:

> *"I am afraid of not satisfying your loved ones, of not being the one they desired for you. I know that you have always been, and still are, the center of their affections, and now I seem to take you away from them, and even though I love them, because they are your dear parents, I do not feel for them that affection which they deserve for the goodness and delicacy they show me."*[121]

Pietro promptly replies, dispelling all doubts:

> *"My dearest Gianna,*
>
> *Your doubt and your fear have no reason to be. For mom, dad, and my sisters I could not find a woman who better than you corresponded to their and my best aspirations, my character, and my life. Mom, dad, and my sisters hoped and desired so much for our 'meeting' and our union long before last December, and they are very happy with our affection, our engagement, and our upcoming marriage. You are the woman my loved ones desired for me."*[122]

---

[120] *Ibid.*

[121] *Ibid.*, letter of 18 April 1955, p. 81.

[122] *Ibid.*, letter of 20 April 1955, p. 81.

Pietro expresses words of esteem for his family of origin; moreover, he motivates what might have seemed to Gianna a concern and distrust with an understandable embarrassment due to not knowing each other and to social status: Pietro's parents were simple people, perhaps intimidated by the cultured and beautiful Doctor Beretta.

> *"Mom and dad are very humble people; excellent people, still made in the best of the old-fashioned mold. They express themselves at ease only in dialect and are completely at ease in their environment. Sometimes, their look, their way of acting may seem worried: having to express themselves in Italian, with people with whom they have not yet full confidence and familiarity, makes them seem awkward, almost concerned to cut a figure, not being up to people, circumstances and places."*[123]

God's Constant Presence

In their epistolary exchange, the reference to God is continuous and constant, a sign of a great faith behind Gianna and Pietro, matured first of all in their families of origin. The two young people's meeting and their love for one another, which is so human, is considered as a grace of God, part of the divine plan in store for them; Gianna writes:

> *"Just think, Pietro, since the Lord has given us this great grace, how grateful we must always be to Him!"*[124]

Pietro prays in his personal prayer after Communion at the first Mass he attends with Gianna:

> *"For the first time we attended Holy Mass together and received Jesus in Holy Communion.*
>
> *'Thank you for giving me Gianna as the sweetest companion*

[123] *Ibid.*, p. 82.
[124] *Ibid.*, letter of 18 April 1955, p. 80.

of my life. Grant that we may always love each other with the strongest, the sweetest, and the purest love. Grant that I may be worthy of her and grant that our family may be blessed by Heaven and be holy in us and in our children': this was my prayer to Jesus as soon as He descended into my heart, while you moved me with your most devout recollection in conversation with Jesus."[125]

Gianna and Pietro recognize that human love has its source in the greatest Love:

"When I think of our great, reciprocal love, I do nothing but thank the Lord. It is quite true that love is the most beautiful sentiment which the Lord has put into the soul of men and women."[126]

It is also deduced that love is such a beautiful feeling that it should not be hidden but in which to rejoice and enjoy:

"But now let us enjoy the joy of loving each other; as I have always been taught that the secret of happiness is to live moment by moment, and to thank the Lord for all that He in His goodness sends us day by day. So let us raise our hearts and live happy!"[127]

In the face of every fear, Gianna also trusts in prayer:

"Lord, You who see my feelings and my good will, make up for my shortcomings, and help me to become a spouse and a mother such as You want and I think that also Pietro desires."[128]

The same is done by Pietro, who invokes and trusts in the Lord

---

125 *Ibid.*, letter of 28 March 1955, pp. 76–77.
126 *Ibid.*, letter of 3 September 1955, p. 87.
127 *Ibid.*, letter of 5 July 1955, pp. 85–86.
128 *Ibid.*, letter of 11 March 1955, p. 70.

to be the kind of man who, as his biography confirmed, he will become, that is, a husband worthy of his holy wife:

> *"I pray to the Lord to make me worthy of you, always."*[129]

Gianna analyzes with extreme realism the uncertain future (no one is immune from difficulties and suffering) but is convinced that their entrustment to God will allow them overcome every obstacle.

> *"It is true, there will also be sorrows, but if we will always love each other as we do now, with God's help, we'll know how to bear them together. Don't you think so?"*[130]

A picture emerges in which, already during their engagement, the upcoming marriage is therefore envisaged as a three-way relationship: Gianna, Pietro, and the Lord as the source and reference point of their love.

> *"Gianna, with the certainty that God wanted us united, you and I have embarked on our new life. In these months it has been all a crescendo of understanding and affection. Now, our understanding is perfect, because Heaven is our light, and the Divine Law is our guide; because Heaven and the Divine Law find in you the most beautiful virtues and the best goodness and in me the very vivid desire and the immense joy to make you always happy. Now our love is full because we are one heart and one soul, one feeling and love, because our love, strong and pure, knows how to wait for the blessing of Heaven."*[131]

This is also confirmed by the proposal Gianna suggested to Pietro to prepare for their marriage:

---

129 *Ibid.*, letter of 21 March 1955, p. 72.
130 *Ibid.*, letter of 5 July 1955, p. 85.
131 *Ibid.*, letter of 10 September 1955, pp. 99–100.

"What would you say if, to prepare ourselves spiritually to receive this Sacrament, we made a triduum? On the 21st, 22nd, and 23rd, Holy Mass and Holy Communion; you at Ponte Nuovo; I at the Shrine of the Assumption."[132]

It is striking that, as the wedding approaches (September 24, 1955), the future bride does not let herself be overwhelmed by the mundane organization, but thinks above all of spiritual preparation; fundamental for Gianna is the participation in Mass and receiving the Eucharist: Jesus, the source of love who died for love.

Pietro accepted with enthusiasm Gianna's proposal by preparing for the "*Sacrament of Love*" in his beloved little church dedicated to Our Lady of Good Counsel in Ponte Nuovo.

The Eucharist is the beating heart of their feeling, so much so that, in their engagement, Gianna and Pietro live a spiritual union that anticipates the sacramental union of marriage.

"Can you believe, I've never enjoyed the Holy Mass and Holy Communion as much as in these days. The little church, so beautiful and recollected, is empty. The Celebrant does not even have an altar boy, so the Lord is all for me, and for you, Pietro, because now where I am, you are also there."[133]

Marriage

From the day of their wedding, an intense and vibrant, albeit brief, married life began. For those who believe that "marriage is the tomb of love," it is sufficient to read the letters that Gianna and Pietro exchanged in those years.

The letters between the spouses are written above all during Pietro's business trips or Gianna's holiday periods in the mountains. In particular, from 26 April to 16 June 1959, Molla the engineer

---

132 *Ibid.*, letter of 3 September 1955, p. 87.

133 *Ibid.*, letter of 23 March 1955, pp. 73–74.

went to the United States of America (to visit various companies producing matches, carbion, molded cellulose packaging, plastic laminates, phosphorus and derivatives, plywood, furniture, paper, and cellulose). Gianna had temporarily moved with the children to her family home in Magenta, where her siblings Francesco, Zita, and Ferdinando, with his family, lived. In these two months, the couple exchanged more than one letter every two days, as if they wished to share everything about those weeks spent apart (as well as postcards, a telegram and tape recordings).

> *"Almost every day, he*[134] *and Mom wrote each other letters, beautiful and very affectionate, which were of great help to them, essential so that they felt close, very close to each other, even if thousands of miles apart."*[135]

The correspondence also offers a cross-section of their daily family life. In addition to the poetic words of love, there are also much more banal and concrete elements: the detailed chronicles of working days, travels, vicissitudes or progress in the children's growth, births and deaths of relatives, friends, and acquaintances; the list of things to take on holiday; even the disappointment for a broken electrical appliance.

The Language of Mature Love

The language of love between Gianna and Pietro does not change its tones of tenderness and affection shown during their engagement; the responsibilities of married, professional, and subsequently parental life do not dim the vivid flame of love between Gianna and Pietro. This can be deduced, in particular, from their greeting cards on the occasion of special anniversaries; in short, incisive sentences,

---

134 Referring to Pietro Molla.

135 From the testimony of daughter Gianna Emanuela in *Gianna Sorriso di Dio,* year 10, nos. 27–28–29, January–December 2011, p. 19.

important words are etched. The following testimonies date back to their first years of marriage:

> *"Pietro my dearest, a year has passed since the day of our engagement: a year of intimate joys, of great love, of full understanding. The most beautiful wish that I wholeheartedly offer you is this: still many, many more years like these, and may the Lord bless and preserve this great love of ours always."*[136]

And again:

> *"With all my love, I wish you*
> *the most wonderful joys,*
> *on your most sweet name day,*
> *the very day that recalls to us our 'yes'*
> *and makes us bless Heaven in the joyful eagerness*
> *of the Divine Gift*[137] *that we are expecting."*[138]

Pietro does not forget, but rather reaffirms the concept of family that Gianna has told him she wants; taking up the words of Gianna herself,[139] her husband confirms:

> *"And I pray again as you prayed that God's help and blessing may make our new family a small Cenacle where Jesus always reigns, as from the day of our marriage to today, over all our affections, desires and actions."*[140]

---

136 Greeting card of 11 April 1956 on their first engagement anniversary, in Gianna Beretta. Pietro Molla, *Lettere*, edited by E. Guerriero, Ed. San Paolo, Cinisello Balsamo (Milan) 2012, p.117.

137 Gianna was expecting Pierluigi, their firstborn.

138 Greeting card of 24 June 1956 on Gianna's name day (the Feast of St. John the Baptist) and their ninth month of marriage, in Gianna Beretta. Pietro Molla, *Lettere*, edited by E. Guerriero, Ed. San Paolo, Cinisello Balsamo (Milan) 2012, p.117.

139 *Ibid.*, letter of 13 September 1955, p. 101.

140 *Ibid.*, letter of 20 December 1955, p.114.

The language of passion, joy, and full feelings between Gianna and Pietro continues in the following years; inspired by the notes of a pianist who performs the piece of light music "*Come prima, più di prima . . . t'amerò*"[141] ['I will love you just as before . . . and even more'], Pietro writes to Gianna, from whom he is far away:

> *"My thought and my heart leapt to you and the music of the piano was the music of my heart and the words that the piano did not speak spontaneously came to my lips and their meaning was full in me. Yes, dearest Little Wife, when I return, I will love you as before, more than before, because I had to stay away from you at a time when, more than ever, you would have desired my company."*[142]

Pietro himself often recalls the happy time spent with his wife, which brings forth new words of admiration for Gianna:

> *"My most beloved Gianna,*
> *I am at the Hotel Des Indes, on the second floor in a room quite identical to the one which put us up in December for our wonderful nights, of kisses and ineffable caresses and very sweet love. You are truly my full and perfect joy, my most beloved and most loving Little Wife!"*[143]

In the letters, there is also space to share and deepen the reflections brought forth by a friar preacher on television. Gianna wants to make her husband part of the teaching:

> *"Last night on TV Father Mariano,*[144] *speaking of the true love of Marriage, said that 'true love is love that does not last a single day, but always' and two spouses who have always loved each*

141 Song made famous by the singer Tony Dallara.

142 Letter of 12 June 1959, in Gianna Beretta. Pietro Molla, *Lettere*, edited by E. Guerriero, Ed. San Paolo, Cinisello Balsamo (Milan) 2012, p. 264.

143 *Ibid.*, letter of 25 January 1961, p. 281.

144 Capuchin Father Mariano da Torino (Paolo Roasenda, 1906–1972), a television preacher.

other, when they are in Paradise will realize that the time they loved each other was short and they will rejoice in thinking that they have all eternity before them, to continue to love each other. Pedrin d'or, you know how much I love you, I think of you, and want you to be happy."[145]

Pietro picks up his wife's cue and responds from New York with words that would seem prophetic, given what happened later with the death of Gianna:

"Father Mariano is perfectly right. Our Love is true Love, and if it has no space limits now, it will not have time limits either."[146]

Mutual esteem and respect are constantly nourished. Husband and wife exchange compliments and thanks, recognizing the virtues of the other. Pietro addresses his wife in this way:

"[. . .] diligent, very attentive and tireless little mom."

Gianna does the same:

"You are truly a dearest and most affectionate little husband, a saintly papa, not of gold, but of diamond, the biggest and most precious one there is on this earth."[147]

and she also thanks her husband for his letters revealing their characteristics:

"[. . .] expressions that reflect your soul, good, sweet, your heart so great, your faith, your spirit of prayer."[148]

---

145 Letter of 13 May 1959, in Gianna Beretta. Pietro Molla, *Lettere*, edited by E. Guerriero, Ed. San Paolo, Cinisello Balsamo (Milan) 2012, pp. 202–203. "*Pedrin d'or*" (diminutive of "Golden Pietro") is a nickname in dialect that the saint often employed to address her husband.

146 *Ibid.*, letters of 16 May 1959, p. 210.

147 *Ibid.*, letter of 4 and 5 June 1959, p. 250.

148 *Ibid.*, letter of 8 June 1959, p. 255.

Gianna, who is pregnant with Mariolina, with Pietro and Pierluigi, Courmayeur, Aosta, Summer 1957.

Pietro's words renew in Gianna the desire to make her husband happy, the identical desire that had characterized their engagement period; thus, Gianna's enthusiasm to always be a good wife and mother does not fade:

> *"I will do everything I can to be always like this, as you want me and see me."*[149]

[149] *Ibid.*, letter of 14 May 1959, p. 206.

Gianna and Pietro never forget that the source of their earthly love is God, the full Love *par excellence*, and, consequently, they thank Him continuously:

> *"And I thank the Lord again for the incomparable gift he has granted me and for the ineffable joys He holds for us and for our family."*[150]

Prayer

Prayer is a fundamental and constant element of the Beretta-Molla family. Beginning with their marriage preparation, it is deduced how strong both spouses' devotion was to the celebration of Holy Mass and the Rosary; in particular, their Marian devotion was very intense, with visits to shrines and local churches, as well as everywhere they went for work or vacation.

> *"We prayed the Rosary every day. In addition, Gianna went to Mass every morning and when she was prevented from doing so, she went to the small Church of Our Lady of Good Counsel for a moment of prayer and meditation. [. . .] We prayed together in the evening before going to bed."*[151]

There are numerous testimonies in their letters; just a few examples of everyday life to demonstrate how much the fidelity to prayer, to the Eucharist, and to Marian devotion were an integral part of their daily life, were its support and point of reference for their thanksgiving:

---

[150] *Ibid.*, letter of Pietro of 25 January 1961, p. 281.

[151] P. Molla - E. Guerriero, *Gianna la donna forte. La beata Gianna Beretta Molla nel ricordo del marito,* Ed. San Paolo, Cinisello Balsamo (Milan) 1995, p. 48.

"This morning I attended Mass and received Holy Communion in our little church, and prayed before Our Lady's beautiful statue for you, Pietro, that she may help you and protect you."[152]

"[I said] a beautiful rosary, the prayer for our family, and with my dear treasure in my heart and in my mind I fell asleep."[153]

"It is to thank Him for all the graces He continually grants us that I go to Church every morning, and to help me to be a good mother and to make you always happy every moment."[154]

"It is now 4:30 a.m., and I am still waiting since 1:45 a.m. for the train with the sleeping car from Stockholm that they announce will arrive only by 5 a.m. Patience. A little discomfort does not hurt. I recite the Holy Rosary."[155]

"In a few moments, I will recite the Holy Rosary, then our usual family prayer and then, as all the previous evenings and the evenings of this trip, before going to bed I will say to Jesus, to the Heavenly Mother and to our Guardian Angels: Bless Gianna and grant that I may be able to make her always happy. Bless the little creature[156] *we are expecting with so much love and so much eagerness. Bless and watch over Pierluigi and Mariolina: protect them from any accident and any illness. May they grow up healthy and good!"*[157]

---

152 Letter of 14 December 1955, in Gianna Beretta. Pietro Molla, *Lettere*, edited by E. Guerriero, Ed. San Paolo, Cinisello Balsamo (Milan) 2012, p. 108.

153 *Ibid.*, letter of 13 December 1955, p. 104.

154 *Ibid.*, letter of 20 July 1958, p. 166.

155 *Ibid.*, letter of 20 December 1955, p. 114.

156 This is their third child, Laura.

157 Letter of 26 April 1959, in Gianna Beretta. Pietro Molla, *Lettere*, edited by E. Guerriero, Ed. San Paolo, Cinisello Balsamo (Milan) 2012, p. 178.

From the correspondence, it is astonishing that Pietro attends Holy Mass even though he is in foreign countries, such as the United States:

> *"This morning I served a Holy Mass at the altar of the Blessed Sacrament of the cathedral of New York, and I attended three other Holy Masses: one for You, one for Gigetto,*[158] *one for Mariolina, and one for the little Creature that we are expecting with such affectionate trepidation."*[159]

Or in nearby Sweden:

> *"Yesterday I received Jesus in the plain but very pious Catholic little chapel of Jönköping from the hands of the excellent Father Ducher, a French Dominican."*[160]

In Sweden, on the occasion of a procession in honor of Saint Lucia, Pietro expresses to his wife some personal considerations on the diversity of religious practices and devotion to the saints:

> *"The songs and Saints of our land speak to us much more to the heart and to the feeling when they are heard and seen in the midst of the Nordic frost: a frost of nature and of religion."*[161]

The Suffering of Distance

Most of their letters are written in periods when Gianna and Pietro had to be apart from one another.

Their desire to be together is obviously constant:

---

158 Gigetto is a term of endearment of their son Pierluigi.

159 Letter of 16 May 1959, in Gianna Beretta. Pietro Molla, *Lettere*, edited by E. Guerriero, Ed. San Paolo, Cinisello Balsamo (Milan) 2012, p. 210.

160 *Ibid.*, letter of 20 December 1955, p. 114.

161 *Ibid.*, letter of 17 December 1955, p. 113.

> *"My dearest Pietro, a night and a half day have passed without my most beloved Pietro: but you are always present to me, and I follow you moment by moment in your long journey. [. . .] Pietro, you will say that I exaggerate: but what emptiness and sadness not to see you!"*[162]

Regret for their distance becomes more acute when Gianna feels in a particular way the nostalgia for Pietro:

> *"Today my ninth month has begun,*[163] *and I tire easily. So, all alone, with joy and great emotion, I read and reread your most affectionate letters, which you have sent me every day from America with so much care. I am in your sweet and dear company, today I am in higher spirits . . . but yesterday, I do not deny it, I felt a bit low. I wished you close, I felt so much nostalgia of you and I had just decided to write to you to come back right away. Then instead . . . it passed me. Today I say to you: 'Come back as soon as possible, Pedrin d'or, as soon as you can.'"*[164]

The difficulty of those days far apart from each other can nevertheless become an offering to God:

> *"Gianna, I offer with you the sacrifice of our distance so that the Lord may continue to bless our dearest and so very beautiful little family."*[165]

Moreover, the regret for being physically separated and distant becomes an opportunity for reflection on the importance which the beloved person now holds. Gianna writes:

---

162 *Ibid.*, letter of 13 December 1955, pp. 103–104.

163 This is her pregnancy of their third child, Laura.

164 Letter of 24 May 1959, in Gianna Beretta. Pietro Molla, *Lettere*, edited by E. Guerriero, Ed. San Paolo, Cinisello Balsamo (Milan) 2012, p. 223.

165 *Ibid.*, letter of 4 May 1959, p. 191.

> *"How much I think of you, Pietro, and now that you are far away, I understand more and more that I love you so much, and that without you I could no longer live."*[166]

Pietro writes, while feeling contrasting sentiments, such as the pain for the distance but also the joy of someone who is waiting for him at home with her affection:

> *"I'm alone, as I am in my many travels; but it is a loneliness which is different from all the other times: it is more painful because now there is you, whom I would always like to have close to enjoy your affection and to make you happy, but it is less disheartening because now there is you, whom I think of every moment, you, who accompany me with your affection, who love me so much, you, to whom I long to return."*[167]

Pietro, making a metaphor with Gianna's professional field, makes a splendid reflection on the distance between lovers, grasping its positive side:

> *"Distance is to love and affection what disease is to health. All the full comfort, the serenity, and the perfect joy that the presence of the loved one gives us are more appreciated when we are far away and are always present to our soul in an atmosphere of profound nostalgia."*[168]

Daily Suffering

In their letters, Gianna and Pietro tell about their daily life, their meetings, their work, and the progress of their days with a wealth of detail.

---

166 *Ibid.*, letter of 14 December 1955, p.108.

167 *Ibid.*, letter of 15 December 1955, pp.111–112.

168 *Ibid.*, letter of 17 September 1957, p.137.

As in any family, there are worries and difficulties to be faced, but Gianna and Pietro are fully aware that they have sworn eternal love before God *in joy and in sorrow, in health and in sickness.*

A mutual attention and a sharing of the sufferings, albeit light, of the other, is deduced.

> *"I'm glad your cough is gone and that your teeth are a bit better. Pedrin d'or, I would wish you never had to suffer anything, or else to be close to you when you are not well."*[169]

Gianna, although she feels badly, wants to share with faraway Pietro every little pain to lighten its burden:

> *"Pietro, forgive me if I am not able to remain silent and not grieve you giving you this news,*[170] *but you are my Pietro, the papa, and by telling it to you, my worries and anxieties become lighter."*[171]

Pietro, for his part, accepts and approves this sharing with his loved one:

> *"It is good that you tell me everything. It is a positive fact, indeed, that when you truly love each other, the joys become greater, and the worries become lighter."*[172]

In this case too, the sufferings (even physical) can become an offering to God:

> *"The heartburn never leaves me, but at least I have some suffering to offer to the Lord for you, my treasure, that you may return soon and safe and sound."*[173]

---

169 *Ibid.*, letter of 11 May 1959, p.200.

170 These are everyday, common burdens linked to their children's health and behavior: Pierluigi's vomiting and Mariolina's crying.

171 Letter of 23 February 1958, in Gianna Beretta. Pietro Molla, *Lettere*, edited by E. Guerriero, Ed. San Paolo, Cinisello Balsamo (Milan) 2012, p. 154.

172 *Ibid.*, letter of 25 February 1958, p. 155.

173 *Ibid.*, letter of 1 June 1959, p. 243.

Pietro shows Pierluigi the little Our Lady located on the outer wall of the holiday home, Courmayeur, Aosta, Summer 1957.

Gianna, who is pregnant with Pierluigi, is knitting, Val Ferret, Courmayeur, Aosta, Summer 1956.

Moments of discouragement, more frequent in Gianna's feminine sensitivity (which is also tried by her ailments), are overcome with faith in God:

> *"[. . .] I do not deny it, Pedrin d'or, that at the news that you cannot return until June 10th, I got a lump in my throat. I had to cry . . . then I offered the sacrifice to the Lord for you, that He may protect you in your continuous flights, and for our popo*[174] *we are expecting,*[175] *so that it may be born beautiful, healthy, without defects; and so . . . I cheered up."*[176]

---

174 The saint often employs the word *popo* or *popi,* meaning 'child' or 'children' in colloquial and dialectal Lombard language.

175 Gianna was expecting Laura, their third child.

176 Letter of 25 May 1959, in Gianna Beretta. Pietro Molla, *Lettere*, edited by E. Guerriero, Ed. San Paolo, Cinisello Balsamo (Milan) 2012, p. 226.

When Gianna is sick from the pregnancy troubles, she declares that precisely her husband's love will be for her a useful support to strengthen her in her soul:

> *"And now Pietro, I ask you a great favor. Please, forgive me if at times you find me in a bad mood, sad: I try to react, but often I am not able; I hope it is an indisposition of these first months. Your great love will help me to be strong."*[177]

It is extremely interesting to note that the saint herself greatly benefits from Pietro's faith. The Christian example, trust in God, and Marian devotion of her husband give her the confidence to face every little tribulation.

> *"Your faith, dearest Pietro, gives me hope in his*[178] *complete healing of a stiff neck."*[179]

The help between Gianna and Pietro is therefore a mutual spiritual help, not just material; the faith that each one nourishes, nourishes the hope and the trust in God within the family. Gianna, who will become a saint, greatly admires her husband from the spiritual point of view, so much so that she wishes to be a good Christian like him; in Pietro, therefore, we cannot but see seeds of holiness, like his wife.

> *"As I have already told you other times, your Faith and your Piety are of great example to me: I would want to be able to pray as you pray, dear Pietro."*[180]

Always, faced with her children's health troubles, Gianna draws strength from her husband's positive attitude:

---

177 *Ibid.,* letter of 11 April 1957, pp.123–124.

178 She is referring to the first born, Pierluigi.

179 Letter of 20 September 1957, in Gianna Beretta. Pietro Molla, *Lettere*, edited by E. Guerriero, Ed. San Paolo, Cinisello Balsamo (Milan) 2012, p.139.

180 *Ibid.,* letter of 22 February 1958, p.151.

"Fortunately, you are more optimistic than me and give me courage, otherwise my morale would almost always be below zero."[181]

What Saint Gianna defines as optimism is explained by Pietro himself not as a natural disposition of his character but as trust in Providence, nourished exclusively by prayer:

"You know: I am optimistic, not by nature; indeed, my disposition and my character would tend somewhat to pessimism. In everything, we can do little, but everything or almost everything depends on Providence and the Lord, such as the health and future of our children and our health; I strive to trust fully and I pray, with as much confidence as possible, to Providence. I obtain a confidence that leads me almost to the intuition and to the certainty that the clouds will dissolve and that the disturbances will remain temporary. That is why I appear to you to be, and I am, optimistic."[182]

These are a few lines, simple and clear, rich only and only of a great faith; the faith of a man of science (graduated in engineering), of a man of great authority and authoritativeness (with prestigious professional appointments), and of a husband who shared with his wife, above all, the love for God and the unconditional abandonment to His will.

Work

Gianna and Pietro were both workers, and one might add, established professionals. Gianna was a pediatrician by vocation, helping people in body and spirit; her commitments were numerous (see 1.2), but she was always able to combine her profession with the

[181] *Ibid.*, letter of 18 February 1958, p.143.
[182] *Ibid.*, letter of 19 February 1958, p.145.

roles of spouse and mother, assisted by family members and domestic helpers. In this regard, her husband testifies:

> *"[. . .] Gianna had asked me to continue her profession as a doctor at least as long as her commitments as a spouse and especially as a mother would have allowed it. I did not object because I knew well the enthusiasm with which she practiced her profession, and her attachment to her patients. Then by mutual agreement we had made the decision that she would have stopped at the birth of our fourth child. With this purpose, she continued her profession until her last admission to the clinic (hospital)."*[183]

In her correspondence with Pietro, Gianna sometimes refers to her work without dwelling on it; the episode in which Gianna brings little Pierluigi with her to work deserves a broader account:

> *"Today I had to take him with me to the Nursery,*[184] *because when he saw me leave the house, he started crying so hard that I couldn't walk away and leave him at home. So, he came with me. He first played a little with the children and with the toys, then he began to call me, and they took him to the medical office; but as soon as he saw me in the medical gown, he became frightened and began to cry . . . Then little by little he adapted to the idea of seeing me dressed this way, and when the children I visited cried, tears came to his eyes. My poor little doctor!!!"*[185]

During the years of their engagement and their marriage, Pietro had already taken on appointments of great working responsibility

---

183 P. Molla - E. Guerriero, *Gianna la donna forte. La beata Gianna Beretta Molla nel ricordo del marito,* Ed. San Paolo, Cinisello Balsamo (Milan) 1995, p. 59.

184 In Ponte Nuovo of Magenta.

185 Letter of 26 February 1958, in Gianna Beretta. Pietro Molla, *Lettere*, edited by E. Guerriero, Ed. San Paolo, Cinisello Balsamo (Milan) 2012, pp.157–158.

at the S.A.F.F.A. Company of Ponte Nuovo (see 2.2). His work commitments were many, his days were busy, and frequent trips abroad were required.

From the beginning of their love story, it is deduced how much Molla the engineer was involved in his work commitments:

> *"I was at the factory and the office today for long hours: from 6:30 a.m. to 8:00 p.m."*[186]

Right from the start, Gianna is aware of her husband's working responsibilities, and, in her great humility, she feels almost guilty for taking away precious time for his rest:

> *"Thank you for the beautiful roses and the hours spent last night in your company. You know, every time I feel the remorse of taking away from you precious time for your rest after a day full of work and worries, as your day is, but on the other hand, I am so happy to be able to enjoy you a little, that I would wish that time would never pass when I am with you."*[187]

When she became his wife, Gianna discreetly laments his excessive work pace and engagement:

> *"Your mother told me yesterday that I shouldn't let you leave, that I should oppose it. 'All words— I replied her—it is part of his duties.' But I said to myself: enough with S.A.F.F.A., let go a bit, you've already done so much!"*[188]

If, on the one hand, Pietro is often tired and far away, on the other hand, he does not fail in his duties as husband and father. As the saint always writes, her spouse is a present and attentive father; moreover, he does not fail to dedicate attentions and affection to his wife.

---

186 *Ibid.*, letter of 21 March 1955, p. 71.

187 *Ibid.*, letter of 11 March 1955, p. 70.

188 *Ibid.*, letter of 9 June 1959, p. 258.

In his letters, Pietro himself admits his excessive work and proposes to change; his desire is always to do more for his family, and he writes several reflections in this regard:

> *"These people from Denmark, Germany and especially England, who are able to finish their work at 5.30-6 p.m. every day and even more so on Saturday, and are able to live long hours in their home, take care of their garden, and enjoy their flowers, taught me to do everything possible to change my habits. And I will strive to treasure this teaching. Especially since you and Pierluigi fully deserve it."*[189]

And again, addressing his family and showing deep humility:

> *"I always think of you; I wish I could always be with you, do much more for you than the little or nothing that I am able to do."*[190]

Pietro also writes in one of his last letters:

> *"The pace of my work and the succession of my travels is really excessive. A change is needed."*[191]

In his last letter sent to Gianna, however, he feels guilty again for not having put his intentions into practice:

> *"I apologize to you if, despite the promises, I am not able to reject the work, when it is beyond the reasonable limit."*[192]

The Support of a Large Family

Gianna and Pietro came from large families. In their marriage and in their married life, they never lacked the support, affection, and closeness from Pietro's mother, brothers, and sisters along with their

---

189 *Ibid.,* letter of 12 April 1957, pp.124–125.
190 *Ibid.,* letter of 9 July 1957, p. 126.
191 *Ibid.*, letter of 15 May 1961, p. 285.
192 *Ibid.*, letter of 13 December 1961, p. 292.

spouses, nieces, and nephews, who were more or less the same age as Gianna and Pietro's children, cousins, and even household helpers.

In numerous letters of their correspondence, there are greetings to the people who gravitated around the couple.

Moreover, in the chronicle of their daily life, news concerning relatives of both Pietro and Gianna's families is often included:

> *"Mom is fine and sends you many, many greetings. She goes to the cemetery, I don't know how many times, to pray for you, for her Pietro. Teresina is better, she only coughs sometimes. Adelaide*[193] *and her family are well too."*[194]

> *"We have with us Fr. Giuse,*[195] *who came to enjoy our little angels a bit. He celebrated Holy Mass in Ponte Nuovo, as usual, and gave a special blessing, with the asperges,*[196] *to our popi and little grandchildren, who also came to their uncle's Holy Mass."*[197]

In the letters, there is no shortage of concerns for family members, for both the minor health troubles of the little ones:

> *"Laura's*[198] *children are well, all fever-free but full of little scabs: they have to stay quarantined for another 15 days, after that, they are free,"*[199]

---

193 This is Pietro's mother; Teresina Villa, Gianna and Pietro's niece as the daughter of Rosetta Molla, and another sister of Pietro.

194 Letter of 14 May 1959, in Gianna Beretta. Pietro Molla, *Lettere*, edited by E. Guerriero, Ed. San Paolo, Cinisello Balsamo (Milan) 2012, p. 206.

195 Fr. Giuseppe Beretta, the saint's brother priest in the Diocese of Bergamo.

196 Gianna refers to the rite of sprinkling holy water.

197 Letter of 10 May 1959, in Gianna Beretta. Pietro Molla, *Lettere*, edited by E. Guerriero, Ed. San Paolo, Cinisello Balsamo (Milan) 2012, p.199.

198 Laura Viola, Gianna's sister-in-law, married to her brother Ferdinando.

199 Letter of 16 July 1958, in Gianna Beretta. Pietro Molla, *Lettere*, edited by E. Guerriero, Ed. San Paolo, Cinisello Balsamo (Milan) 2012, p.164.

and for the problems related to the fatigue of the older ones:

> *"Luigia*[200] *was very happy to be able to spend some recreation with me. As usual, she confided a little. The essential, not to say the only, cause of her headaches, poor digestion and downheartednesses, is, in my opinion, too much work that never leaves her a moment of rest and recreation at any time of the day and on any day of the year. Since last week, the sisters [in her convent], who had always been 7, have been reduced to 5, as two more were needed in Borgio Verezzi. Luigia is resigned to it because, she says, such is convent life."*[201]

During Pietro's long journey to the United States, Gianna moved into her home in Magenta with her siblings Francesco (called Cecco) and Zita. Moreover, her sister Zita helped the saint a lot, even in her spousal home in Ponte Nuovo, with the daily things and caring for the little children; her presence was a cause for concern for Gianna, who thought she could be seen by her husband as an interference in their family life.

> *"Do you regret that Zita continues to come to help me for a little more time? I ask you this, dear Pietro, because at times I have the doubt that you are not happy."*[202]

Pietro responds the next day, confirming his "*Anything but*" written instinctively in the margin of the same letter sent by his wife.[203]

---

200 Sister Luigia Molla, Pietro's sister and nun at the Congregation of the Most Precious Blood, was the director of the *Sorriso d'Italia* boarding school in Imperia; Pietro, who was in Sanremo for a period of rest due to overwork and fatigue, had gone to visit her.

201 Letter of 22 February 1958, in Gianna Beretta. Pietro Molla, *Lettere*, edited by E. Guerriero, Ed. San Paolo, Cinisello Balsamo (Milan) 2012, p.153.

202 *Ibid.*, letter of 18 February 1958, p.143.

203 *Ibid.*, see footnote 100, p.143.

"I am very, very happy and I greatly appreciate the precious help that the good Zita gives you, as a true and very attentive Godmother."[204]

Another occasion to bring together the large Beretta-Molla family was the summer holidays; from the letters written from the holiday resorts, it emerges that the visits of siblings and in-laws with nephews and nieces were frequent and welcome, to reconstruct even on vacation, that welcoming and open family atmosphere that already existed in everyday life:

"Today, instead, we spent the day at Checrouit:[205] *we woke up this morning with a wonderful sunshine, a clear sky and not at all cold. We prepared our backpacks and luggage, and to the great joy of Flavio and Gianfranco,*[206] *we took the cableway and went up."*[207]

"Adelaide, Cecco and Zita left half an hour ago, refreshed a little and happy to have spent a day with their nice little grandchildren."[208]

Or:

"Laura[209] *and her children came today; Pierluigi, Mariolina and Lauretta showed them every detail of our little house, inside and out, with great enthusiasm."*[210]

---

204 *Ibid.*, letter of 19 February 1958, p.146.

205 Hill overlooking Courmayeur, located in the Aosta Valley.

206 Flavio and Gianfranco Valenti, nephews of Gianna and Pietro, are Adelaide Molla's sons.

207 Letter of 18 July 1957, in Gianna Beretta. Pietro Molla, *Lettere*, edited by E. Guerriero, Ed. San Paolo, Cinisello Balsamo (Milan) 2012, p.134.

208 *Ibid.*, letter of 20 July 1958, p.166.

209 Laura Viola, Gianna's sister-in-law, married to her brother Ferdinando.

210 Letter of 4 July 1960, in Gianna Beretta. Pietro Molla, *Lettere*, edited by E. Guerriero, Ed. San Paolo, Cinisello Balsamo (Milan) 2012, p. 274.

Pietro with Gianna and her siblings: Ferdinando, Father Alberto and Zita; Pietro's mother, Maria Salmoiraghi; Pietro's sister, Adelaide, with her husband, Vittorio Valenti, and their sons, Gianfranco and Flavio, Ponte Nuovo of Magenta, 1959.

Even the household helpers seem to be part of the family; in fact, the greetings included in the letters of the two spouses are often addressed to them; they are Liberata Villa, the domestic helper for over fifty years at the Beretta house ("*An affectionate greeting to Zita, Cecco, Nando and family and to Liberata*"[211]) and Savina Passeri, the domestic helper in Gianna and Pietro's house from 1956 to 1962 ("*Cordial greetings to Savina*"[212]). A colorful note involves precisely Mrs. Savina; the saint, opening her heart with her husband in a letter, expounds a certain divergence in her educational methods, which are perhaps more hasty:

> "*Angela*[213] *is just very attentive and capable and knows how to help them play and takes care of them really well. If it*

[211] *Ibid.*, letter of Pietro of 27 April 1959, p.179.

[212] *Ibid.*, letter of Pietro of 25 July 1958, p.171.

[213] Angela Chiolerio, Gianna's friend.

were Savina as it is Angela! How much a little schooling and patience mean!"[214]

It should be remembered, however, that the Beretta-Molla family always had esteem for their helper, who offered a beautiful testimony during the beatification process.

Savina Passeri also stated:

"I started working with Mr. and Mrs. Molla when I was nineteen years old. I didn't know how to do much, but Mrs. Gianna never scolded me. She was very patient. If sometimes I raised my voice with the children, because they were teasing each other, Mrs. Gianna requested me to be calmer: 'They are small,' she told me. 'We must teach them to be good, without shouting.' And she was fair to her children. She knew how to correct them when they were up to some mischief."[215]

The Fear (and Poetry) of Flying

Another colorful note arising from their correspondence is the fact that Saint Gianna had a great fear of airplanes, despite the fact that she herself had traveled (by plane). Knowing that her husband was flying, Beretta was anxious every time Pietro had to fly:

"[...]at last, only this morning, I could learn that your plane had arrived in Boston, after a nine-hour delay. Last night at nine o'clock I phoned the TWA management in Milan, but they only had news until 3 p.m. You can imagine the kind of hours we have spent."[216]

---

214 Letter of 8 May 1959, in Gianna Beretta. Pietro Molla, *Lettere*, edited by E. Guerriero, Ed. San Paolo, Cinisello Balsamo (Milan) 2012, p.197.

215 G. Pelucchi, *L'amore più grande. Santa Gianna Beretta Molla,* Ed. Paoline, Milan, 2004, pp. 137–138.

216 Letter of 28 April 1959, in Gianna Beretta. Pietro Molla, *Lettere*, edited by E. Guerriero, Ed. San Paolo, Cinisello Balsamo (Milan) 2012, p.180.

Reports of two plane crashes put Gianna in a state of further apprehension.

> *"From today's newspaper, we learn that two planes crashed in the U.S.: one New York-Atlanta near Baltimore, the other while landing at the airport of Kanwha (Virginia); both four-engine 'Capital Airlines.' My Pietro, you can imagine how my thoughts are always with you, with your travels, and how I wish that the day when you have finished flying come soon. It is good that there is the trinomial of Gigetto, who every time he prays says: 'Jesus, grant that my daddy may have a good journey; that daddy may come back soon; that daddy may not fall.' But . . . distance is always distance."*[217]

Therefore, because he was aware of Gianna's fear, Pietro preferred to travel by train; travel times and comforts are not the same as a plane, and Gianna knows this perfectly:

> *"I'm sorry it is so hot and that to make me happy you must get tired traveling hours and hours by train. Patience, Pedrin d'or, but I am calmer knowing you are not in 'heaven.'"*[218]

It also makes one smile that the saint shows herself to be concerned about the characteristics of the aircraft used by her husband, making her considerations as an apprehensive wife:

> *"Going back to your flights, are two-engine airplanes safe? Excuse my ignorance, but it seems to me that a four-engine can better withstand air pockets, etc., etc."*[219]

---

217 *Ibid.*, letter of 13 May 1959, p. 202.

218 *Ibid.*, letter of 14 May 1959, pp. 205–206.

219 *Ibid.*, letter of 25 May 1959, p. 227.

Her tone, however, immediately returns to being affectionate and romantic, with a reference to the divine and another to the communion of their family:

> *"I enjoy, however, in reading that it was an enchanting journey for you, close to the pilot, and close to Heaven! And since we too are always with you, it is as if we too enjoy all the beautiful things that you always tell us about."*[220]

Pietro, for his part, reassures his wife by entrusting of them to the divine aid:

> *"I fly safely on the wings and on the strength of your Prayers and those of our Treasures,"*[221]

and, in a joking tone, on the responsibility of men who have to account for the precious good of their family:

> *"Mr. O'Connor said last night to me that the greatest security we had on Wednesday on the American Cyanamid plane was not the radar, but the fact that the Pilot had six young children at home who are always waiting for him!"*[222]

"The Prayer of My Flights"

Precisely during one of his flights, within the already mentioned period of work in the United States, Pietro composed a prayer of extraordinary intensity and beauty.

"*'The prayer of my flights' is truly magnificent,*" said his daughter Gianna Emanuela.[223] The context is that of a spectacular aerial journey over an extremely suggestive natural landscape, capable of inspiring praise to the Creator.

---

220 *Ibid.*

221 *Ibid.*, letter of 26 May 1959, p. 228.

222 *Ibid.*, letter of 28 May 1959, p. 233.

223 *Ibid.*, from Gianna Emanuela Molla's preface to the letters of her father, p. 18.

"Most beloved Gianna,

I am flying in a splendid sky—at an altitude of 6,000 meters—over the Rocky Mountains and the Grand Canyon of Colorado and Utah. It is a spectacle that I will never forget: eroded mountains, rising straight up from the rivers and valleys, rivers that wear the rock away and snake through it: green rivers and blue lakes; rocks ranging from golden yellow to scarlet red and to dark copper red. It is a sight of a power that I did not expect.

And in this sky and above these rocks that sometimes break down into a desert of red sand and that speak more than ever of the power and the Providence of the Creator, I repeat the prayer of my flights. I begin it at this moment when we are between heaven and rock, and I have here before me the marvelous pictures of you and of our Treasures whom I kiss in this same heaven."[224]

It is a poetic composition in some passages, in which Pietro puts the members of his family at the center of his prayers.

"Jesus, who created me and who preserves me amidst graces and blessings without limits: You who between my distant flights now in time and those of today, in these same Heavens, have given me the immense gift of a Wife of gold, like the most marvelous dawn that only up here can be admired, and of two Treasures, splendid as the Heaven in its full brightness that can only be embraced from on high; You who will soon give to us again the divine gift of another Treasure, hear my prayer:

Bless Gianna and our Treasures! Transform into graces their anxiety and trepidation for my long staying far away and my flights.

224 *Ibid.*, letter of 31 May 1959, p. 239.

Listen, today and always, to the Prayers of Gianna, of my Gigetto, of my Mother and of all those who love me! Look upon the little folded hands of my Mariolina! Give me the grace of a joyful return!

And grant that at every moment I may advance always in Your Way, just as the plane flies, precisely, on course, safe, radio-controlled.

May I always have the holy Fear of You, as that which can be felt up here, where I am more than ever entrusted to your divine Providence, sustained on the wings of the prayers of Gianna, of my Treasures, of my Mother and of all those who pray for me.

Grant that the serene and bright atmosphere of the sky through which I am flying at this moment may always reign over our family; the purity of the clear air I breathe.

Grant that the clouds may just skim over us and leave us quickly, like the small clouds up here.

Keep my family and my dear ones joyful and serene in Your Way and in Your Light, today and until the day we will fly up, up, higher and higher, up to You. Amen."[225]

The engineer addresses Jesus directly, thanking Him implicitly for "*graces and blessings without limits*"; Jesus who gave him ("*the immense gift*") of a wife, two children, and a third on the way; he compares the members of his family to natural elements, connected to the sight from the plane ("*Wife of gold, like the most marvelous dawn that only up here can be admired,*" and again, referring to Pierluigi and Mariolina as "*two Treasures, splendid as the Heaven in its full brightness that can only be embraced from on high.*"). Pietro asks for divine blessing on his family, that Jesus would listen to the devoted prayers of his loved ones and for the success of his journey. The "aeronautical" comparison that Pietro makes between his conduct as a good Christian and the plane is certainly noteworthy; it is

225 *Ibid.*, letter of 31 May 1959, pp. 239–240.

an image of great intensity and, at the same time, fruit of progress and modernity; indeed, he asks the Lord that he may always remain in His straight path ("*Your Way*") just as an airplane travels safely and precisely on its radar-marked course. Pietro also asks to renew in himself the Fear of God just as he feels it more weighty at that time, in flight, in which he feels more vulnerable and entrusted to Providence. The prayer continues with the request for graces for his family, always inserting aerospace metaphors: Pietro invokes a serene and clear atmosphere such as that perceptible at a high altitude and compares, implicitly, the difficulties of daily life to clouds; these are clouds/problems that he is aware there will be, but for which he trusts in a rapid dissolution. Pietro Molla's ode closes with the invocation to preserve his family and dear ones in joy and serenity until death, seen as an ascent to heaven, toward God ("*until the day we will fly up, up, higher and higher, up to You.*").

Parenthood

The love relationship between Gianna and Pietro finds complete fulfilment and total realization in the birth of their four children; the deep feelings between the two spouses become visibly concrete in the flesh of four creatures: Pierluigi, Maria Zita, Laura, and Gianna Emanuela. Precisely their deep awareness of being givers of life will lead Gianna, and Pietro silently in agreement with her, to give their own existence in order to allow their last daughter to come into the world.

The Desire to be Parents

Gianna and Pietro, as already emphasized, wished to have children, many children. Since both were in love with life, they were enthusiastic to give life to other creatures.

Already during their engagement period, trusting in this gift, Gianna writes:

"Think, Pietro of our nest, warmed by our affection and made joyful by the beautiful 'popi' that the Lord will send us!"[226]

The same feeling dwells in the heart of Pietro, who was traveling for work:

"In the children of Sweden, who also say 'Mamma' as in our language, I foresaw the gifts of Heaven, your jewels, O Gianna, the children that God wants to give us in blessing and joy."[227]

It was a desire that was not an end in itself or for personal satisfaction; being givers of life and Christian educators was seen by Gianna (and shared by Pietro) as a role within God's creative project:

"We become God's collaborators in His creation, so we can give Him children who love Him and serve Him."[228]

Life is a gift, not taken for granted and immediate, so Gianna and Pietro always entrust themselves to prayer to God and to Marian devotion; Pietro even composes a prayer for his future family:

"O Lord and our Heavenly Mother bless our Love and make it fruitful! May the day come soon when Gianna, happier than ever before, can share with me and our loved ones the holy announcement that a new life lives in her! After this coming Christmas, may the next Christmases see our children in prayer before the Baby Jesus! Give us the grace and the joy, O Lord, O Heavenly Mother, to bring our children before your altars and to consecrate them to You! Keep us, O Lord, always eager, like the Sacred Family of Nazareth, for the holy education of our children!"[229]

---

226 Letter of 5 July 1955, in Gianna Beretta. Pietro Molla, *Lettere*, edited by E. Guerriero, Ed. San Paolo, Cinisello Balsamo (Milan) 2012, p. 85.

227 *Ibid.*, letter of 10 September 1955, pp. 98–99.

228 *Ibid.*, letter of 13 September 1955, p.101.

229 *Ibid.*, letter of 13 December 1955, pp.105–106.

The Gift of Life

Gianna's first maternity brings forth in the future parents words of great consideration for the new child in their family, called by Pietro: "*The Divine Gift that we await*"[230] and "*The sweetest Fruit of our Love.*"[231]

Their joy for their firstborn Pierluigi renews their desire to enlarge their family; daddy Pietro declares, in a letter to his wife, that he is writing a diary in the form of a colloquy with his little son, and that he has written him:

> *"May Heaven give us again the immense, divine grace of a treasure like you: a little sister or little brother!"*[232]

Therefore, it emerges that Gianna and Pietro consider the life of their children a gift and a grace from God; each of their children, on the day of their baptism, was also consecrated to Our Lady of Good Counsel of (the small Church in) Ponte Nuovo, a sanctuary so dear to the married couple, who lived nearby.

New pregnancies are not long in coming anyway; Gianna writes:

> *"The Lord has again blessed our love by giving us another child: I am happy, and with the help of the Heavenly Mother and with you close to me, with you who are so good, understanding and affectionate, I am no longer afraid of the sufferings of the new maternity."*[233]

As already mentioned, Gianna suffered considerable indispositions during each pregnancy; this did not prevent her, however, from being open to life.

---

230 *Ibid.*, from Pietro's greeting card for Gianna's name day, 24 June 1956, p. 117.

231 *Ibid.*, from Pietro's greeting card on their first wedding anniversary, 24 September 1956, p. 118.

232 *Ibid.*, letter of 7 April 1957, p. 122.

233 *Ibid.*, letter of 11 April 1957, p. 123.

Apprehension and trust in Providence therefore accompany every maternity, even the last one which will later prove to be the most painful and the fatal one in God's plan:

> *"I know that you are a strong woman in suffering and that you know how to hide your worries. I also know that you prefer and wish that I not be anxious about you; but I almost never manage not to let myself be overcome with anxiety. Stay very serene, Gianna dearest, you will see that even this fourth Maternity will be blessed and happy like the others that preceded it!"*[234]

Moreover, Gianna's children had various health troubles, all curable, of which a detailed chronicle can be obtained (hip dislocation, hyperesthesia of the first tract of the pharynx, stiff neck . . . in addition to seasonal diseases). Despite her profession as a pediatrician, which allowed her to easily solve the problems by scientifically analyzing the medical cases and consulting her best colleagues, Gianna shares in and takes upon herself the suffering of her children when they are sick, like all mothers:

> *"Dear Pietro, I would never have imagined that we would have to suffer so much to become mothers! I would like to see them [the children] always beautiful, without any trouble that can make them suffer, and instead every day there is a little thorn."*[235]

The joy of being mothers, givers of life, however, surpasses every tribulation; Gianna reiterates this (referring to the experience of her cousin Piera, who had a "*magnificent baby girl*" after having "*had to suffer a lot*" from a caesarean section):

> *"The Lord immediately consoles us mothers, doesn't He?"*[236]

---

234 *Ibid.*, letter of 13 December 1961, p. 292.

235 *Ibid.*, letter of 18 February 1958, p.143.

236 *Ibid.*, letter of 29 May 1959, p. 235.

The Mutual Esteem as Parents

Even in their role as parents, Gianna and Pietro do not tarnish their language of mutual esteem for the role they have assumed by opening to life. There are numerous attestations of affection involving their fatherhood and motherhood. Pietro addresses Gianna with endearments full of appreciation for her daily maternal task:

> *"[. . .] Little Mom all love, all sweetest cares."*[237]

> *"He is now practically cured of his cold, thanks to his little mom's wise cares."*[238]

> *"A thank you and an infinite gratitude for the joy you have always given me and for being the incomparable Little Mom of our Treasures."*[239]

Gianna also has words of deep consideration for her husband as a father:

> *"What a dear little husband and what a holy dad our children have!"*[240]

Moreover, the aforementioned expression that Gianna dedicates to Pietro after receiving his letter with the "*The prayer of my flights*" included must be remembered; it is a note placed at the end of the letter, after the greetings, almost like a *post scriptum* dictated by love:

> *"[. . .] a saintly papa, not of gold, but of diamond, the biggest and most precious one there is on this earth."*[241]

---

237 *Ibid.,* letter of 31 January 1957, p.119.

238 *Ibid.,* letter of 17 September 1957, p.136. Pietro refers to little Pierluigi.

239 *Ibid.,* letter of 24 July 1958, p.168.

240 *Ibid.,* letter of 18 July 1957, p.134.

241 *Ibid.,* letter of 4 June 1959, p. 250.

Initiation into Prayer

"She also taught the children to pray. Unfortunately, she died when they were still little, but she has immediately directed them to prayer,"[242] as Pietro testifies.

The joy and conviction that grew in the Beretta-Molla spouses through the practice of prayer are also passed on to their children. In particular, it is deduced from the letters how Gianna taught the prayers and the gestures of devotion to her children. She writes to Pietro, referring to Pierluigi:

"[. . .] I often made him recite the Hail Mary and the Eternal Rest prayer, his two favorite prayers that he knows well by heart."[243]

The little ones are also taught to ask for the intercession of deceased loved ones while visiting the cemetery:

"Yesterday morning I took the popi to Mesero to the Cemetery, to the graves of grandfather and aunt Teresina;[244] *they prayed for you with their little folded hands, that all goes well."*[245]

Deep Marian devotion is also passed down to the little ones:

"[. . .] Our wonderful popi wanted to stop at the Sanctuary,[246] *each light a candle, one lit by Pierluigi and one lit by Mario-*

---

242 P. Molla - E. Guerriero, *Gianna la donna forte. La beata Gianna Beretta Molla nel ricordo del marito,* Ed. San Paolo, Cinisello Balsamo (Milan) 1995, p. 48.

243 Letter of 28 April 1959, in Gianna Beretta. Pietro Molla, *Lettere*, edited by E. Guerriero, Ed. San Paolo, Cinisello Balsamo (Milan) 2012, p.181.

244 They are Pietro's relatives: his father Luigi, deceased in 1956, and his sister Teresina, who died in 1950.

245 Letter of 8 May 1959, in Gianna Beretta. Pietro Molla, *Lettere*, edited by E. Guerriero, Ed. San Paolo, Cinisello Balsamo (Milan) 2012, p.197.

246 This is the Aosta Valley Sanctuary of Notre Dame de la Guérison in Val Veny, at the foot of Mont Blanc, and two kilometers from downtown

lina, and recite with their little folded hands a Hail Mary for their Little Mom far away."[247]

"Pierluigi always recites the Ave (Maria) for his daddy and ends with 'may daddy come back soon'"[248]

In the correspondence, Gianna sometimes writes greetings and thoughts to Pietro as if his children were writing directly to him:

"Dearest daddy, thank you for the postcard, for thinking of us, for all your very affectionate words. We are sorry you are not here with us, to enjoy the beautiful sunshine and the beautiful snow of Courmayeur! We are having so much fun. Thank you, daddy, for bringing us up here!"[249]

Pietro himself addresses his children directly, telling them about his journey and gifts for them:

"Dearest Gigetto and Mariolina,

Daddy is here in the land of hunting and the ancient Redskins. I'll bring you a nice Cowboy outfit.

On the plane with Daddy, there are many children.

Daddy kisses you very, very much and You kiss Mommy for me."[250]

Sometimes it is Pierluigi himself, the eldest son, who writes a greeting with a childish and uncertain hand;[251] this practice is a way to make faraway Pietro feel the closeness of the children, but it is also

---

Courmayeur, the family's holiday resort.

247 From a postcard from Courmayeur (where Pietro was on holiday without Gianna) of 13 July 1960, in Gianna Beretta. Pietro Molla, *Lettere*, edited by E. Guerriero, Ed. San Paolo, Cinisello Balsamo (Milan) 2012, p. 277.

248 *Ibid.*, letter of 29 April 1959, p.184.

249 *Ibid.*, postcard of 14 February 1961, p. 282.

250 *Ibid.*, postcard of 30 May 1959, p. 237.

251 *Ibid.*, letter of 8 June 1959, p. 256, and letter of 16 May 1959, p. 208.

an educational way that Gianna had to pass on to the children the gratitude and the affection toward their father.

Gianna and Pietro with Pierluigi, Mariolina, and Laura,
Courmayeur, Aosta, Summer 1960.

7
The Message Today of an Exemplary Couple

FROM what has emerged from the analysis of the marital, familiar, and parental journey of Gianna Beretta and Pietro Molla, it is possible to see in this couple an example for all Christians who embrace the spousal vocation of love for the other. The Church is constantly looking for positive examples to show how holiness can be lived in everyday life, even as spouses, workers, and parents.

> *"Knowing that marriage and the family constitute one of the most precious of human values, the Church wishes to speak and offer help to those who are already aware of the value of marriage and the family and seek to live it faithfully, to those who are uncertain and anxious and searching for the truth, and to those who are unjustly impeded from living freely their family lives."*[252]

In particular, it seems that the marital journey of Gianna and Pietro is a precursor of the concept of spousal relationship inaugurated at the Second Vatican Council and continued with the other documents of the Magisterium; even the Archbishop of Milan, Cardinal Angelo Scola, has emphasized:

---

[252] Saint John Paul II, *Familiaris Consortio,* Apostolic Exhortation on the Role of the Christian Family in the Modern World, 22 November 1981, no. 1.

> *"[. . .] Precisely the Council convoked by John XXIII and brought to completion by Paul VI favored that new vision of the relationship between man and woman and of marriage in Christ, of which there is an anticipatory trace in their correspondence."*[253]

Engagement

From what has emerged from their writings, Gianna and Pietro live their engagement as a time of grace: from the human point of view, to know each other and share their principles from the spiritual point of view, to strengthen their faith and prepare themselves for the sacrament of marriage.

Making a comparison with the Second Vatican Council, the council texts barely mention the theme of engagement, but it is possible to find in them affinities with the practice already expressed by Gianna and Pietro. Paragraph 49 of *Gaudium et Spes*, the Pastoral Constitution (7 December 1965) of the Second Vatican Council, emphasizes:

> *"The biblical Word of God several times urges the betrothed and the married to nourish and develop their wedlock by pure conjugal love and undivided affection."*

Gianna and Pietro also constantly drew inspiration from the Word of God to build up their relationship; in particular, Gianna referred to the female figures set forth in Sacred Scripture, such as the virtuous woman in the final alphabetical (short) poem of the Book of Proverbs 31:10–31.

The two, as an engaged couple, had already placed the Lord at the center of their relationship, to whom they both always turn with

---

[253] From the presentation of Cardinal Angelo Scola to the book Gianna Beretta. Pietro Molla, *Lettere*, edited by E. Guerriero, Ed. San Paolo, Cinisello Balsamo (Milan) 2012, pp.6–7.

great gratitude for the gift of each other; their authentic sentiment leads them spontaneously to God, as Benedict XVI reminds engaged couples:

> *"The experience of love has within it a movement towards God."*[254]

Gravitating around God, the relationship between Gianna and Pietro is based on prayer and, in particular, on the Eucharist; they had already intuited that this sacrament is the source of human love, and they frequented the Eucharist assiduously, entrusting their love in the celebration of the Eucharist during Mass, both on the day of their official engagement and in their triduum of marriage preparation:

> *"The Eucharist is the very source of Christian marriage. The Eucharistic Sacrifice, in fact, represents Christ's covenant of love with the Church, sealed with His blood on the Cross (cf. Jn 19:34). In this sacrifice of the New and Eternal Covenant, Christian spouses encounter the source from which their own marriage covenant flows, is interiorly structured and continuously renewed."*[255]

From the testimonies, it emerges, in particular, the complementarity of their characters: Gianna, sunny and involving people in every activity, even playful; Pietro, more reserved and dedicated to work; it seems to find, even in their personalities, that original complementarity of which St. John Paul II also speaks in the apostolic exhortation *Familiaris Consortio*:

> *"This conjugal communion sinks its roots in the natural complementarity that exists between man and woman, and is*

---

254 Meeting with Engaged Couples, Ancona, 11 September 2011.

255 Saint John Paul II, *Familiaris Consortio,* Apostolic Exhortation on the Role of the Christian Family in the Modern World, 22 November 1981, no. 57.

> *nurtured through the personal willingness of the spouses to share their entire life-project, what they have and what they are.*"[256]

For Gianna and Pietro, the presence of their own families of origin is also extremely important, not only for the transmission of the faith but also for the support in their vocational journey; Gianna's family members (with her spiritual director) had persuaded her not to leave for Brazil as a missionary but rather to emulate her mother as a family woman; the saint (who, when she became engaged to Pietro, was already an orphan of both parents) shows moreover her concern (which was unfounded) of not liking her in-laws and sisters-in-law. These attitudes recall *Gaudium et Spes* no. 59, where the idea is expressed that parents are the best guides in the discernment and responsibility of the specific vocation of their children, as well as *Apostolicam Actuositatem* no. 11, which exhorts spouses to "prudently help them [the children] in the choice of their vocation," and recalls also that "among the various activities of the family apostolate is that of helping engaged couples to prepare themselves better for marriage."

In the initial phase of their correspondence, the language of Gianna and Pietro is the enthusiastic language of those falling in love; as time passes, the love between the two is not touched, on the contrary, it seems to become more mature and rooted in their sensitivity and will. Almost sixty years later, the example of Gianna and Pietro seems to be found in the words of Benedict XVI at the World Meeting of Families in Milan (2012):

> "*[. . .] This loving sentiment is a wonderful thing, but it has to be purified, it has to undergo a process of discernment, that is, reason and will have to come into it. Reason, sentiment and will have to come together. In the Rite of Marriage, the Church does not say: 'Are you in love?' but 'Do you wish?' 'Have you*

---

256 *Ibid.*, no.19.

decided?' In other words, falling in love has to become true love by involving the will and the reason in a deeper journey of purification which is the journey of engagement, such that the whole person, with all his or her faculties, with the discernment of reason and strength of will, says: 'Yes, this is my life.'"[257]

Marriage

The official beginning of the recent renewal of Catholic doctrine on marriage and the family is recognized in *Gaudium et Spes*, in particular, in the first chapter of the second part, entitled "Fostering the Nobility of Marriage and the Family" (nos. 47–52). We are therefore chronologically a few years after the death of Saint Gianna, but in it we can find a similarity with the ideal of marriage that Gianna and Pietro put into practice. In particular, the Molla spouses have demonstrated how the essence of marriage is in the "*intimate community of life and conjugal love*;" their desire to give themselves for the happiness of the other is moreover a sign of that "*covenant between spouses, a human act by which the spouses mutually give themselves and receive each other.*"

From their first intentions, Gianna and Pietro's family plans to be "*a small cenacle where Jesus reigns over all our affections, desires, actions.*"[258]

The two spouses desire and make it so that their Christian family is the place of the primacy of Jesus. Their example must enlighten Christian families of yesterday and today:

"In our own time, in a world often alien and even hostile to

---

257 Benedict XVI, address at the Evening of Witness, 7th World Meeting of Families, Saturday, 2 June 2012, Bresso Park (Milan).

258 Expression Gianna employed in her letter of 13 September 1955, in Gianna Beretta. Pietro Molla, *Lettere*, edited by E. Guerriero, Ed. San Paolo, Cinisello Balsamo (Milan) 2012, p.101, and by Pietro in his letter of 20 December 1955, *Ibid.*, p. 114.

> *faith, believing families are of primary importance as centers of living, radiant faith."* [259]

This ideal of the family as a small domestic church, anticipated in the letters of the spouses, is already made clear by the Second Vatican Council in *Lumen Gentium* n. 11:

> *"Finally, Christian spouses, in virtue of the sacrament of Matrimony, whereby they signify and partake of the mystery of that unity and fruitful love which exists between Christ and His Church (cf. Eph. 5:32) help each other to attain to holiness in their married life and in the rearing and education of their children. By reason of their state and rank in life they have their own special gift among the people of God. From the wedlock of Christians there comes the family, in which new citizens of human society are born, who by the grace of the Holy Spirit received in baptism are made children of God, thus perpetuating the people of God through the centuries. The family is, so to speak, the domestic church. In it parents should, by their word and example, be the first preachers of the faith to their children; they should encourage them in the vocation which is proper to each of them, fostering with special care vocation to a sacred state."*

The same concept is found in the Pope Saint John Paul II's Exhortation *Familiaris Consortio*:

> *"The Christian family is also called to experience a new and original communion which confirms and perfects natural and human communion. In fact, the grace of Jesus Christ, 'the first-born among many brethren,' (Rom 8:29) is by its nature and interior dynamism 'a grace of brotherhood,' as St. Thomas Aquinas calls it (Summa Theologiae, II-II, q. 14, art. 2, ad 4). The Holy Spirit, who is poured forth in the celebration of the*

---

259 *Catechism of the Catholic Church*, no.1656.

sacraments, is the living source and inexhaustible sustenance of the supernatural communion that gathers believers and links them with Christ and with each other in the unity of the Church of God. The Christian family constitutes a specific revelation and realization of ecclesial communion, and for this reason too it can and should be called 'the domestic Church.'"[260]

And again:

"The Christian family too is part of this priestly people which is the Church. By means of the sacrament of marriage, in which it is rooted and from which it draws its nourishment, the Christian family is continuously vivified by the Lord Jesus and called and engaged by Him in a dialogue with God through the sacraments, through the offering of one's life, and through prayer."[261]

Between Gianna and Pietro, there is a deep esteem and, above all, a great respect; even from their correspondence, it emerges that the spouses are convinced of the equal dignity of man and woman, as masterfully explained in *Familiaris Consortio*:

"Authentic conjugal love presupposes and requires that a man have a profound respect for the equal dignity of his wife: 'You are not her master,' writes St. Ambrose, 'but her husband; she was not given to you to be your slave, but your wife. . . . Reciprocate her attentiveness to you and be grateful to her for her love' (Exameron, V, 7, 19: CSEL 32, I, 154)."[262]

Gianna and Pietro always treat each other as equals; an equality in dignity and a diversity in the identity of man and woman, father and mother, which enriches their relationship and their being:

---

260 Saint John Paul II, *Familiaris Consortio,* Apostolic Exhortation on the Role of the Christian Family in the Modern World, 22 November 1981, no. 21.

261 *Ibid.*, no. 55.

262 *Ibid.*, no. 25.

Gianna and Pietro, engaged, Livigno, Sondrio, August 4th, 1955.

> *"In their fruitful relationship as husband and wife, in their common task of exercising dominion over the earth, woman and man are marked neither by a static and undifferentiated equality nor by an irreconcilable and inexorably conflictual difference. Their most natural relationship, which corresponds to the plan of God, is the 'unity of the two,' a relational 'uni-duality,' which enables each to experience their interpersonal and reciprocal relationship as a gift which enriches, and which confers responsibility."*[263]

Prayer

A fundamental element of Gianna and Pietro's married life is prayer; thanksgiving and entrustment to God, given to them by their families of origin and cultivated through their belonging to Catholic Action, are cornerstones in this couple's daily life. This

263 Saint John Paul II, *Letter to Women,* 29 June 1995, no. 8.

practice seems to be reaffirmed, in 1981, in the Apostolic Exhortation *Familiaris Consortio*:

> *"[. . .] far from being a form of escapism from everyday commitments, prayer constitutes the strongest incentive for the Christian family to assume and comply fully with all its responsibilities as the primary and fundamental cell of human society."*[264]

Gianna and Pietro seem to have already understood what Saint John Paul II explained in his *Letter to Families,* referring to Saint Paul:

> *"Marriage, the Sacrament of Matrimony, is a covenant of persons in love. And love can be deepened and preserved only by Love, that Love which is 'poured into our hearts through the Holy Spirit which has been given to us' (Rom 5:5)."*[265]

From the correspondence, it emerges that each episode (positive or negative) of family life can be the object of a prayer, can become a reason for thanksgiving, entrustment, or an offering pleasing to God; the description of family prayer made by St. John Paul II therefore seems to correspond perfectly to that of Gianna and Pietro.

> *"Family prayer has for its very own object family life itself, which in all its varying circumstances is seen as a call from God and lived as a filial response to His call. Joys and sorrows, hopes and disappointments, births and birthday celebrations, wedding anniversaries of the parents, departures, separations and homecomings, important and far-reaching decisions, the death of those who are dear, etc.-all these mark God's loving intervention in the family's history. They should be seen as suitable moments for thanksgiving, for petition, for trusting*

264 Saint John Paul II, *Familiaris Consortio,* Apostolic Exhortation on the Role of the Christian Family in the Modern World, 22 November 1981, no. 62.
265 Saint John Paul II, *Letter to Families,* 2 February 1994, no.7.

abandonment of the family into the hands of their common Father in heaven."[266]

Gianna and Pietro, as husband and wife, constantly continue their participation (as daily as possible, even in foreign countries) in Holy Mass to receive the Eucharist.

"The Eucharist is the very source of Christian marriage. The Eucharistic Sacrifice, in fact, represents Christ's covenant of love with the Church, sealed with His blood on the Cross (cf. Jn. 19:34). In this sacrifice of the New and Eternal Covenant, Christian spouses encounter the source from which their own marriage covenant flows, is interiorly structured and continuously renewed. As a representation of Christ's sacrifice of love for the Church, the Eucharist is a fountain of charity. In the Eucharistic gift of charity, the Christian family finds the foundation and soul of its 'communion' and its 'mission.'"[267]

A precious reference point for their married life is also the recitation of the Holy Rosary, of which there is often testimony in their correspondence as a habitual practice in the context of a profound Marian devotion; again, we find the words of *Familiaris Consortio*:

"While respecting the freedom of the children of God, the Church has always proposed certain practices of piety to the faithful with particular solicitude and insistence. Among these should be mentioned the recitation of the rosary: "We now desire, as a continuation of the thought of our predecessors, to recommend strongly the recitation of the family rosary. . . . There is no doubt that . . . the rosary should be considered as one of the best and most efficacious prayers in common that the Christian family is invited to recite. We like to think, and sincerely hope, that

---

266 Saint John Paul II, *Familiaris Consortio,* Apostolic Exhortation on the Role of the Christian Family in the Modern World, 22 November 1981, no. 59.

267 *Ibid.*, no. 57.

when the family gathering becomes a time of prayer the rosary is a frequent and favored manner of praying" (Saint Paul VI, Apostolic Exhortation Marialis Cultus, 52-54: AAS 66 (1974), 160 s.). In this way authentic devotion to Mary, which finds expression in sincere love and generous imitation of the Blessed Virgin's interior spiritual attitude, constitutes a special instrument for nourishing loving communion in the family and for developing conjugal and family spirituality. For she who is the Mother of Christ and of the Church is in a special way the Mother of Christian families, of domestic Churches."[268]

It must be emphasized that the love between Gianna and Pietro does not fade with the passage of time; on the contrary, their feelings become more mature and aware. The comparison made by Benedict XVI is well suited to the example given by Gianna and Pietro:

> *"I often think of the wedding-feast of Cana. The first wine is very fine: this is falling in love. But it does not last until the end: a second wine has to come later, it has to ferment and grow, to mature. The definitive love that can truly become this 'second wine' is more wonderful still, it is better than the first wine. And this is what we must seek. Here it is important that the 'I' and the 'you' are not alone, but that the parish community is also involved, the Church, the circle of friends. All this—the right degree of personal maturity, communion of life with others, with families who support one another—is very important, and only in this way, through this involvement of the community, friends, the Church, the faith, God himself, can a wine emerge that will last forever."*[269]

---

268 *Ibid.*, no. 61.

269 Benedict XVI, address at the Evening of Witness, 7th World Meeting of Families, Saturday, 2 June 2012, Bresso Park (Milan).

Work

Gianna and Pietro were both workers and esteemed professionals.

Pietro, in his correspondence, often expresses his regret for being far away or too busy because of work and his desire to take more time for his family. Gianna also discreetly complains about Pietro's excessive commitments but recognizes his qualities as a father and husband. The figure of Pietro seems to find fulfillment in the words of Saint John Paul II about the man as spouse and father; in a context of work and of great responsibilities, Pietro does not fail in the full realization of his vocation as husband and father.

> *"Love for his wife as mother of their children and love for the children themselves are for the man the natural way of understanding and fulfilling his own fatherhood. Above all where social and cultural conditions so easily encourage a father to be less concerned with his family or at any rate less involved in the work of education, efforts must be made to restore socially the conviction that the place and task of the father in and for the family is of unique and irreplaceable importance" (cf. Saint John Paul II, Homily to the Faithful of Terni (March 19, 1981), 3-5: AAS 73 (1981), 268-271).*[270]

As for Gianna, it has already been remembered that the saint was one of the few women doctors of the time; she put her work skills at the total service of the neediest. In love with her work, she did not abandon it despite having three children to raise. In Gianna the worker, we find the portrait evoked by Saint John Paul II in his *Letter to Women* (29 June 1995), no. 2:

> *"Thank you, women who work! You are present and active in every area of life: social, economic, cultural, artistic, and*

[270] Saint John Paul II, *Familiaris Consortio,* Apostolic Exhortation on the Role of the Christian Family in the Modern World, 22 November 1981, no. 25.

> *political. In this way you make an indispensable contribution to the growth of a culture which unites reason and feeling, to a model of life ever open to the sense of 'mystery,' to the establishment of economic and political structures ever more worthy of humanity."*

Gianna is an extremely emancipated woman in the cultural context of the 1950s and 60s, combining a demanding job and the family. The saint anticipates the guidelines set forth by Saint John Paul II:

> *"There is no doubt that the equal dignity and responsibility of men and women fully justifies women's access to public functions. On the other hand, the true advancement of women requires that clear recognition be given to the value of their maternal and family role, by comparison with all other public roles and all other professions. Furthermore, these roles and professions should be harmoniously combined, if we wish the evolution of society and culture to be truly and fully human."*[271]

Parenthood

Gianna tells Pietro that she wants children in order to be "*collaborators*" in God's creative work. That was in their engagement period in 1955; in 1981, Saint John Paul II made explicit the same concept of parents as "*cooperators in the love of God the Creator*":

> *"Thus, the fundamental task of the family is to serve life, to actualize in history the original blessing of the Creator—that of transmitting by procreation the divine image from person to person."*[272]

The great love between the Molla spouses becomes a source and an example of love also for their children. Gianna and Pietro, as

271 *Ibid.*, no. 23.

272 *Ibid.*, no. 28.

emerges from their correspondence, are aware that the source of human love is always and only God.

Gianna and Pietro's marriage is fruitful; every child is accepted as a blessing, every life is a gift from God to defend and promote.

Gianna, who faced her six pregnancies despite health troubles, also seems to perfectly embody the description of "*woman who is a mother*" evoked by Saint John Paul II:

> *"Thank you, women who are mothers! You have sheltered human beings within yourselves in a unique experience of joy and travail. This experience makes you become God's own smile upon the newborn child, the one who guides your child's first steps, who helps him to grow, and who is the anchor as the child makes its way along the journey of life."*[273]

Every child is also a person to raise and educate. The Second Vatican Council recalls in the document *Gravissimum educationis*, n. 3:

> *"Since parents have given children their life, they are bound by the most serious obligation to educate their offspring and therefore must be recognized as the primary and principal educators."*

After having welcomed their children with joy, Gianna and Pietro are aware they must educate them in the best possible way, transmitting Christian values to them:

> *"For Christian parents the mission to educate, a mission rooted, as we have said, in their participation in God's creating activity, has a new specific source in the sacrament of marriage, which consecrates them for the strictly Christian education of their children: that is to say, it calls upon them to share in the very authority and love of God the Father and Christ the Shepherd, and in the motherly love of the Church, and it enriches them with wisdom, counsel, fortitude and all the other gifts of*

---

[273] Saint John Paul II, *Letter to Women,* 20 June 1995, n. 2.

> *the Holy Spirit in order to help the children in their growth as human beings and as Christians."*[274]

The "*educational mission*" of Gianna and Pietro together, toward their children, is very brief; Gianna dies when their firstborn Pierluigi was not yet six years old, Mariolina was four and a half, and Laura just under three. From their correspondence, however, it is possible to outline how Gianna and Pietro had already begun to trace a spiritual educational path for their children, transmitting to them the foundations of faith and prayer.

> *"Certainly, one area in which the family has an irreplaceable role is that of religious education, which enables the family to grow as a 'domestic church.' Religious education and the catechesis of children make the family a true subject of evangelization and the apostolate within the Church. We are speaking of a right intrinsically linked to the principle of religious liberty. Families, and more specifically parents, are free to choose for their children a particular kind of religious and moral education consonant with their own convictions. Even when they entrust these responsibilities to ecclesiastical institutions or to schools administered by religious personnel, their educational presence ought to continue to be constant and active."*[275]

Every child of the couple received the sacrament of Baptism with a special consecration to Our Lady of Good Counsel (of the small Church) of Ponte Nuovo of Magenta. From the very beginning, daily prayer has been a constant of the relationship between the two fiancés, who then became spouses; a prayer of praise and invocation that becomes familiar, that is, proper to the Beretta-Molla family, which recognizes in God the matrices of every life and every

---

274 Saint John Paul II, *Familiaris Consortio,* Apostolic Exhortation on the Role of the Christian Family in the Modern World, 22 November 1981, no. 38.

275 Saint John Paul II, *Letter to Families,* 2 February 1994, no. 16.

affection. Gianna and Pietro, in the simplicity of the transmission of faith in their family, are once again a concrete example of what the documents of the Magisterium and the Popes recommend:

> *"By reason of their dignity and mission, Christian parents have the specific responsibility of educating their children in prayer, introducing them to gradual discovery of the mystery of God and to personal dialogue with Him: 'It is particularly in the Christian family, enriched by the grace and the office of the sacrament of Matrimony, that from the earliest years children should be taught, according to the faith received in Baptism, to have a knowledge of God, to worship Him and to love their neighbor' (Gravissimum Educationis, 5; cf. Saint John Paul PP. II, Catechesi Tradendae, 36).*
>
> *The concrete example and living witness of parents is fundamental and irreplaceable in educating their children to pray. Only by praying together with their children can a father and mother-exercising their royal priesthood-penetrate the innermost depths of their children's hearts and leave an impression that the future events in their lives will not be able to efface. Let us again listen to the appeal made by Paul VI to parents: "Mothers, do you teach your children the Christian prayers? Do you prepare them, in conjunction with the priests, for the sacraments that they receive when they are young: Confession, Communion and Confirmation? Do you encourage them when they are sick to think of Christ suffering, to invoke the aid of the Blessed Virgin and the saints? Do you say the family rosary together? And you, fathers, do you pray with your children, with the whole domestic community, at least sometimes? Your example of honesty in thought and action, joined to some common prayer, is a lesson for life, an act of worship of singular value. In this way, you bring peace to your homes:* Pax huic domui. *Remember, it is*

thus that you build up the Church" (General Audience Address, 11 August 1976: Teachings of Paul VI, XIV (1976), 640)."[276]

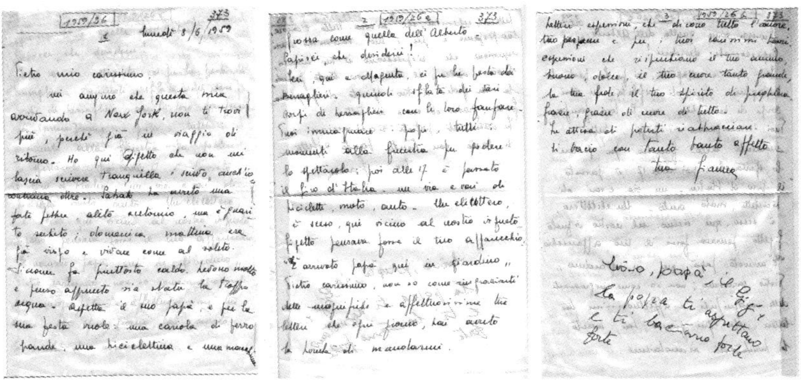

Letter of Gianna to Pietro, June 8th, 1959.

From what emerges from their correspondence, they teach their children the prayers and pass on to them the principal foundations of the Christian faith; given the age of the children, their conscious participation in Holy Mass, of course, is premature, even if Gianna took them with her to church.

---

276 Saint John Paul II, *Familiaris Consortio,* Apostolic Exhortation on the Role of the Christian Family in the Modern World, 22 November 1981, no. 60.

Gianna and Pietro married, Basilica of Saint Martin, Magenta, September 24th, 1955

Conclusion

IN today's society, in which the role of the family is often mistreated and devalued in its importance for society as a whole, the correspondence of Gianna Beretta and Pietro Molla casts a light of hope on the revaluation of the feeling of love between man and woman and on the life-project connected to it. This plan begins with their engagement, then it is realized with the sacrament of marriage and their subsequent openness to life, in being parents understood as givers of life, educators, and initiators in the faith through their example.

The analysis of their correspondence has allowed a thorough examination of different aspects of the marital journey of Saint Gianna and her husband; initially, however, we wanted to frame the biography of the protagonists, Gianna Beretta and Pietro Molla, bringing out the fundamental importance of their families of origin, an example of authentically Christian families.

Gianna and Pietro's life together, which lasted only seven years in all, has been reported in its three main stages: engagement, marriage, and parenthood, through the biographical facts and the very words of the protagonists and of the witnesses.

We therefore proceeded to study in depth the correspondence between Gianna and Pietro, an extraordinary testimony of their relationship. The three main areas of investigation have been the time of their engagement, their marriage, and their parenthood. For each section we tried to highlight some of the most significant aspects, such as, first of all, the poetic language of the fresh (young) love, of the mature love, and of the mutual esteem as parents. In the section on their engagement, we also emphasized Gianna's ideal of a wife and of Christian family, and her concrete and understandable fears related to her insertion in the family of origin of her future husband; the already constant presence of God, as fruit of the education by their families of origin and of a conscious and mature choice by Gianna and Pietro, first of all as single persons, and then as a Christian couple. In the section on their marriage, we examined the themes of the daily endurance of suffering, both ordinary and extraordinary (for their distance because of business trips); and of the consideration of their own work and of the relationship with their family of origin. Their testimony about prayer is precious, it is the fundamental element on which Gianna and Pietro's marriage is based, and, inspired by Gianna's fear when her husband was on an airplane, the brief analysis of "*The Prayer of my flights*" written by Pietro himself. In the section on their parenthood, we studied in depth the themes of the desire and the profound respect for life, and the themes of the initiation of their little children into prayer and faith.

The messages of Gianna and Pietro gathered from their letters (divided into the themes of engagement, marriage, prayer, work, and parenthood) were then compared with the documents of the Magisterium. It is extraordinary to note how much the two spouses are forerunners of what was drafted by the Second Vatican Council and recommended by the Popes in the following years. This anticipation and analogy are based on their common will to refer themselves always and in every way to the teaching of Jesus. Gianna and Pietro did nothing but put into practice what they had learned from the pages of Sacred Scripture and the Gospel.

Some considerations therefore emerge.

The Example

What emerged from their correspondence can be a valid, and above all concrete, example for today's young people who are approaching Christian engagement time and marriage. Already in testimonies and meetings for engaged couples and spouses, speakers use the letters of Saint Gianna and Pietro, as their children Pierluigi, Laura, and Gianna Emanuela always have done, who are called to spread the values embodied not only by their holy mother but also by their father, her worthy spouse. From the letters, a conception of love understood as a gift emerges, a free gift of the totality of oneself in response to an appeal that comes from the other; love is presented not as a possessive relationship, because the other is not an object of property, but as a relationship that implies reciprocity and responsibility toward the other person. Gianna and Pietro testify with their words, set down in black and white, of how the engagement period must be lived for every Christian couple: as a precious period in which to deepen their relationship, to learn to know each other better, to question themselves about their vocation, that is, to ask themselves how to love each other and how to love God and others through their love. Gianna and Pietro testify, with their words, to consider the sacrament of marriage as a possibility to become an image of the covenant of love between God and man, between Christ and the Church; through this sacrament, by virtue of the action of the Holy Spirit, Gianna and Pietro became an icon, a true image of Christ's union with the Church. The mutual conviction of Gianna and Pietro was to make their family a "*cenacle*," a *domestic church*, in which the teaching of Jesus reigned above all things, and which could become a witness of Christ in society. The vocation of Gianna and Pietro continues with their natural and resolute openness to life: the life of new creatures is desired, respected, educated, initiated into the faith but above all loved to the end, to Gianna's sacrifice that inevitably involved Pietro, willing to renounce the future with his spouse and the unity of his family.

The Holiness

Gianna and Pietro are the example of how the love between two persons and their plan to be a family can be a condition within which to develop holiness. We all are called to become "*honest citizens and saintly Christians.*"[277]; this goal can be achieved in every sphere, and in every social, economic, and cultural condition. In particular, holiness is attainable in the frequent daily role of husband, wife, and parents. What Gianna and Pietro communicate to each other, despite having been written more than fifty years ago, is extremely topical because it is an expression of authentic feelings and of a will to build every relationship and every future plan on the teachings of the Gospel. Saint Gianna rose to the honors of the altars as a doctor, wife, and exemplary mother: the insertion in the working world, the relationship of a couple, and parenthood are three characteristics that pertain to the majority of Christians, and this shows how sanctity can be attained in daily life. The entire life of Gianna, whose vocation as a wife and

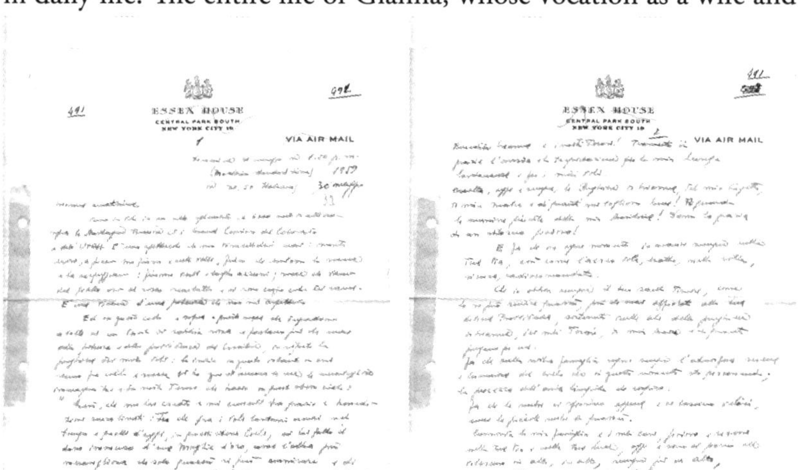

Letter of Pietro to Gianna, May 31th, 1959.

277 From the teaching of Saint John Bosco.

mother is outlined in the letters, was set according to the principles of the Gospel; her gesture to give her own life to save that of the baby girl she carried in her womb was therefore the worthy conclusion of an extraordinarily ordinary existential journey.

Pietro

Gianna's example is worthily supported by her husband Pietro: the figure of engineer Molla is absolutely not to be underestimated. Indeed, the analysis of their correspondence has led, in certain situations, to make him shine almost more than his holy spouse. It is Pietro, for example, who has the most poetic words to express his love for Gianna. He shares and nurtures every aspect of the family spirituality set forth with Gianna: the constant prayer of invocation and praise, the regular participation in the Eucharist sought even when abroad for work, the desire to form an authentically Christian family, the ability to accept difficulties by entrustment to God, and the openness to the gift of life. It is amazing that the saint is inspired by Pietro as a model of prayer and faith. Common logic would lead us to think the opposite; instead Saint Gianna found precisely in her husband the model and the strength to continue in a strong faith, so strong even to the gift of herself. One should therefore speak not of a married saint but of a holy couple. Gianna and Pietro are the example of how it is possible to become a holy couple in everyday life as professionals, spouses, and parents.

To conclude, it must be remembered that the sacrament of marriage between Gianna and Pietro did not last only for seven years on earth but for almost fifty years after Gianna's death. Pietro Molla never wanted to remarry, recognizing in Gianna the exclusivity of the only woman prepared by the Eternal Father for him, the only woman who could complete him and enhance him in his dignity as a man, and who could be an incomparable wife and mother. With the passing of Engineer Molla, the marriage of Gianna and Pietro will endure forever, confirming the Scripture:

> "*. . . For Love is strong as Death,*
> *longing is fierce as Sheol.*
> *Its arrows are arrows of fire,*
> *flames of the divine.*
> *Deep waters cannot quench love,*
> *nor rivers sweep it away.*"[278]

---

278 Canticle of Canticles 8:6–7.

D
J

Gianna and Pietro during their honeymoon,
St. Peter's Square, Rome, September 25th, 1955.

APPENDIX

THE LORD BLESSED ME WITH TWO "SAINT PARENTS"

By Gianna Emanuela Molla [279]

A FEW months after my Mom entered Heaven, my Dad wrote a long letter to my uncle Father Alberto, his brother-in-law, of whom he was very fond, who lived in Brazil. The letter ends with this very beautiful prayer:

> *"Dearest Father Alberto, . . . Every day, since Gianna ascended to Heaven, I raise this prayer to the Lord and to Gianna: "Jesus, You who have called among your Angels and your Saints, my Spouse and the Mother of my children, grant that even today my children may grow up in wisdom and grace with You, with Our Lady, with their Holy Mother, with their loved ones and with men, just as You grew up in Your Holy Family in Nazareth, and just as their Holy Mother knew how to bring them up, day by day. Keep them in health of mind and body, just as their Holy Mother, with Your grace and Your blessing, knew how to preserve them with her wise, very loving care.*

[279] Final part of the testimony on Saint Gianna Beretta Molla, given on 21 September 2018, in Lugano (Switzerland) by her daughter Gianna Emanuela, on the occasion of the Intensive Study Week organized by the Faculty of Theology of Lugano, entitled *Women and the Church: Motherhood, Prophecy, Theology*; the complete testimony is published in the *Theological Review of Lugano* of the Faculty of Theology, year XXIV, no. 1, March 2019, pp. 165–179.

Grant that my children may always be worthy, every day of their lives, of the Holiness and Martyrdom of their Holy Mother. Grant that I may be the least unworthy as possible of the Holiness of my Spouse, and that I may replace her, by Your grace, in the lovingness and guidance of our children. Grant also to me and my children the grace, the certainty, and the ineffable comfort that made Saint Augustine write of his Holy Mother in Heaven: "When you were alive, I saw you where you were. Now that you are in Heaven, I feel you present wherever I am."

And you, Gianna, help me day by day, to carry my Cross, to accomplish, in a heroic way, the will of the Lord. May you obtain also for our children and for me the divine grace to make us saints.

Grant that every day may bring us nearer to you, and that every day we may climb a rung of Jacob's mystical ladder, at the top of which you are awaiting us. And grant that when the Lord will call us to Himself, He may find us worthy to come near, near, near to you forever. Amen."

I lived 48 years of my life with my Dad and I can testify that my Mom has heard his prayer: she has helped him, day by day, to carry his cross, and to accomplish, in a heroic way, the will of the Lord; and when the Lord called him to Himself he was more than worthy to live with her forever!

According to His will, my parents lived their married and family life together for only six and a half years, then Mom flew to Paradise; during the 48 years that Dad lived without her visible presence, they continued to be "*one heart and one soul,*" spiritually very united and in communion: true love, which is love that lasts forever, really is much stronger than death!

I remember that my Dad prayed a great deal, and that he continued to thank the Lord, for everything; I was struck by the fact that, although he had suffered tremendously in his long life, he always said to me: "*Eternity will not be enough for me to thank the Lord for all the graces He has granted me in my long life,"* referring, in particular, to the grace of having been able to be present at the proclamation of my Mom as a Saint by Pope Saint John Paul II in St. Peter's Square in Rome.

When he passed away on April 3, 2010, Holy Saturday, Cardinal Carlo Maria Martini, Archbishop Emeritus of Milan, sent my family a handwritten note with these words:

> *"From my heart I participate in the mourning for the death of Engineer Molla, who was the Spouse of Saint Gianna. She will have welcomed him into paradise with great joy, just as Easter approaches."*

Since that Holy Saturday, I think of my most beloved "Dad of gold"—his Gianna lovingly called him: "*Pedrin d'or*"—forever united with his adored Spouse and my most beloved Mom; I always feel them close, even better, "clinging" to me, to protect me and to guide my steps; I turn to them continually with my prayers, and I feel that they listen to me.

More and more people, from various parts of the world—cardinals, bishops, priests, consecrated persons, including cloistered nuns, and lay people—tell me and write to me that the Lord has blessed me with two "*saint parents*," that Gianna and Pietro are two "*saint spouses*," and that they pray to them asking for their intercession. On the other hand, as can be read in the letters she wrote to him, it has been precisely my Mom who first recognized the sanctity of my Dad, and who followed his example; now that she has been proclaimed a "Saint" by the Church, her words acquire an even greater meaning and value.

On the occasion of Lent 2014, the Parish of St. Gregory the Great in Milan invited me to comment on the last four Stations of the *Via Crucis*, asking me, in particular, to develop this theme: *What does my Parents' life teach me about the Way of the Cross.* I confess that it was not easy for me: I prayed and asked for the help of the Holy Spirit to enlighten me, and these reflections were born.

The life of my holy parents teaches me that "*the Way of the Cross*" is certainly the right way that I must follow, in order to be able to attain, one day, to enjoy the joy of Paradise, the joy of the vision of God, and forever.

The way of the Cross, closely united and indissoluble from that of the Resurrection, as our Lord Jesus testified and showed, is humanly the most uncomfortable and the most difficult; however, I think it is the only way that allows us to give a full and complete meaning to our life.

It presupposes, as our Heavenly Mother has taught us well, our unconditional and continuous "Yes" to the Father's will, our humble acceptance of His holy will, always and anyway, even when we do not understand it.

The life of my holy parents teaches me that "*the Way of the Cross*" is certainly also "the way of joy," the truest and deepest joy, the prelude to that even greater and deeper joy of being able to enjoy one day the vision of the Lord, and forever . . .

And to have the Lord in our heart, to fulfill His holy will, to see every single thing that happens to us in the light of faith, leads us, while walking on the way of the Cross, to the joy, and to feel the duty to thank, and continuously, our Lord, for everything, for our every breath—as my Dad taught me—for His every single gift . . . even for that of suffering.

And whenever a "new" suffering comes, even very heavy, of those sufferings that happen like "a bolt from the blue" and that, despite them, come as a grace to strengthen you in faith, I think: "*I am on the right way . . .*," and this thought encourages me and helps me very much to accept it, and little by little, with the help of Heaven and those close to me, to face it and to "overcome" it, if we can say so, as much as humanly possible, always thinking of the greatest Good and the greatest Joy that await me . . .

To conclude, I would like to tell you that every morning, when I wake up and open my eyes, after having given thanks for the gift of life I pray to the Lord, to the Virgin Mary and to Saint Joseph to help me to be the least unworthy as possible of my Parents. I am living with the joy and the hope of being able to embrace them again, together with Mariolina and all my other loved ones, one day, and, this time, forever, to never leave each other again!

I assure you of my daily prayer, according to all the intentions you have in your heart; I ask you the kindness to pray for me and for my mission, and I thank you again for inviting me here, to give my testimony: it has truly been a great honor and a great joy for me.

Gianna and Pietro during their honeymoon, Naples, September 1955.
Mariolina, 1963.

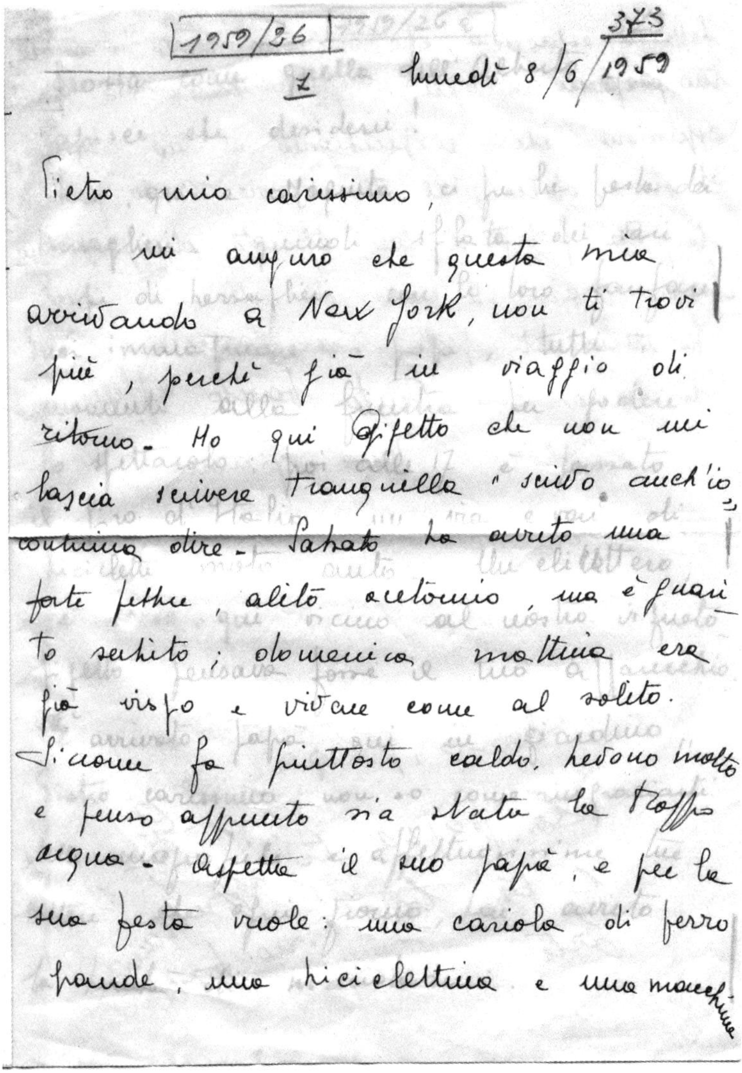

1959/26 | 373

1 lunedì 8/6/1959

Pietro mio carissimo,

mi auguro che questa mia arrivando a New York, non ti trovi più, perchè già in viaggio di ritorno. Ho qui Pipetto che non mi lascia scrivere tranquilla "scrivo anch'io" continua a dire. Sabato ha avuto una forte febbre, alito acetonico, ma è guarito subito; domenica mattina era già vispo e vivace come al solito. Siccome fa piuttosto caldo, bevono molto e penso appunto sia stata la troppa acqua. Aspetta il suo papà, e per la sua festa vuole: una cariola di ferro grande, una biciclettina e una macchinina

Letter of Gianna to Pietro, June 8th, 1959. (seen on p. 127)

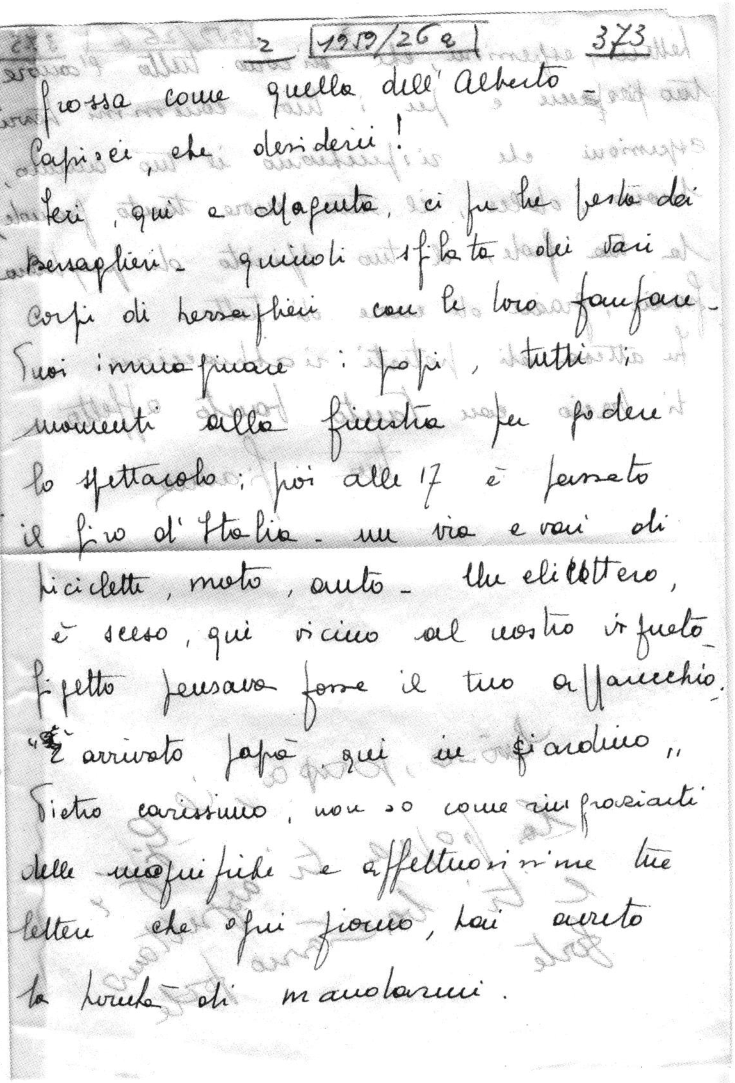

2 [1959/26 a] 373

grossa come quella dell'Alberto -
Capisci, che desiderii!
Ieri, qui a Magenta, ci fu la festa dei
bersaglieri - quindi sfilata dei vari
corpi di bersaglieri con le loro fanfare.
Puoi immaginare: pupi, tutti i
momenti alla finestra per godere
lo spettacolo; poi alle 17 è passato
il giro d'Italia - un via e vai di
biciclette, moto, auto - Un elicottero,
è sceso, qui vicino al nostro in fondo -
Pietro pensava forse il tuo apparecchio.
"È arrivato papà qui in giardino"
Pietro carissimo, non so come ringraziarti
delle magnifiche e affettuosissime tue
lettere che ogni giorno, hai avuto
la bontà di mandarmi.

Letter of Gianna to Pietro, June 8th, 1959. (seen on p. 127)

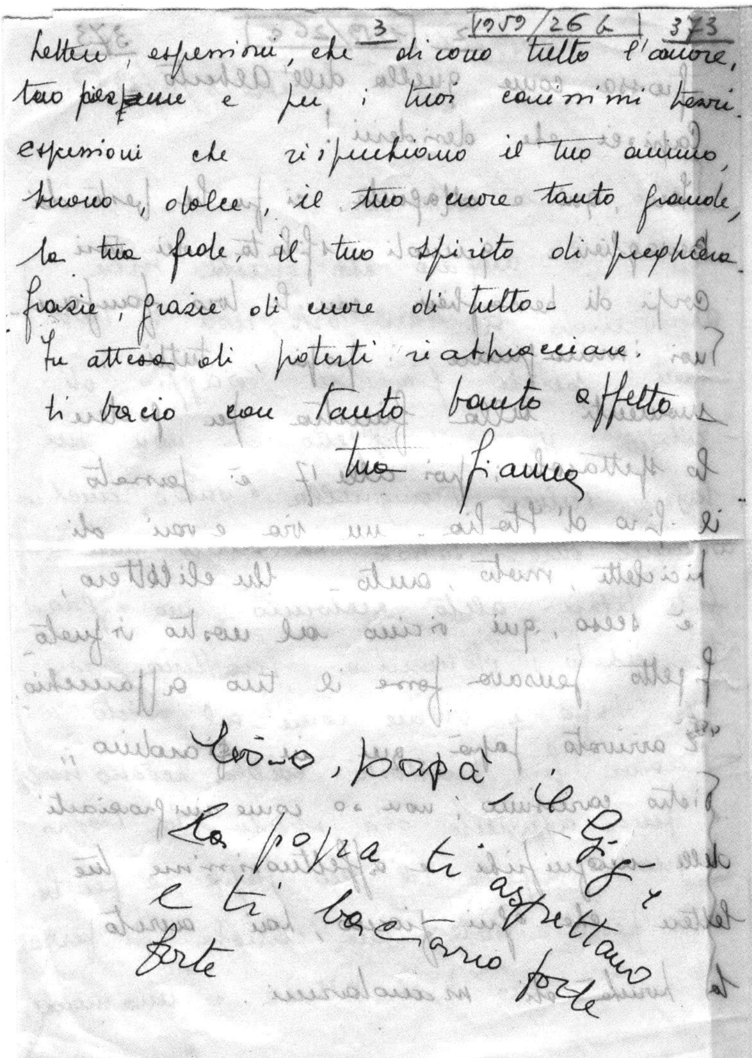

3 1959/266 373

lettere, espressioni, che dicono tutto l'amore, tuo pensiero e per i tuoi cari mi mi tenevi. espressioni che rispecchiano il tuo animo, buono, dolce, il tuo cuore tanto grande, la tua fede, il tuo spirito di preghiera. Grazie, grazie di cuore di tutto. In attesa di poterti riabbracciare ti bacio con tanto tanto affetto

tua Gianna

Ciao, papà, il Gigi la Pozza ti aspettano e ti baciano forte forte

Letter of Gianna to Pietro, June 8th, 1959. (seen on p. 127)

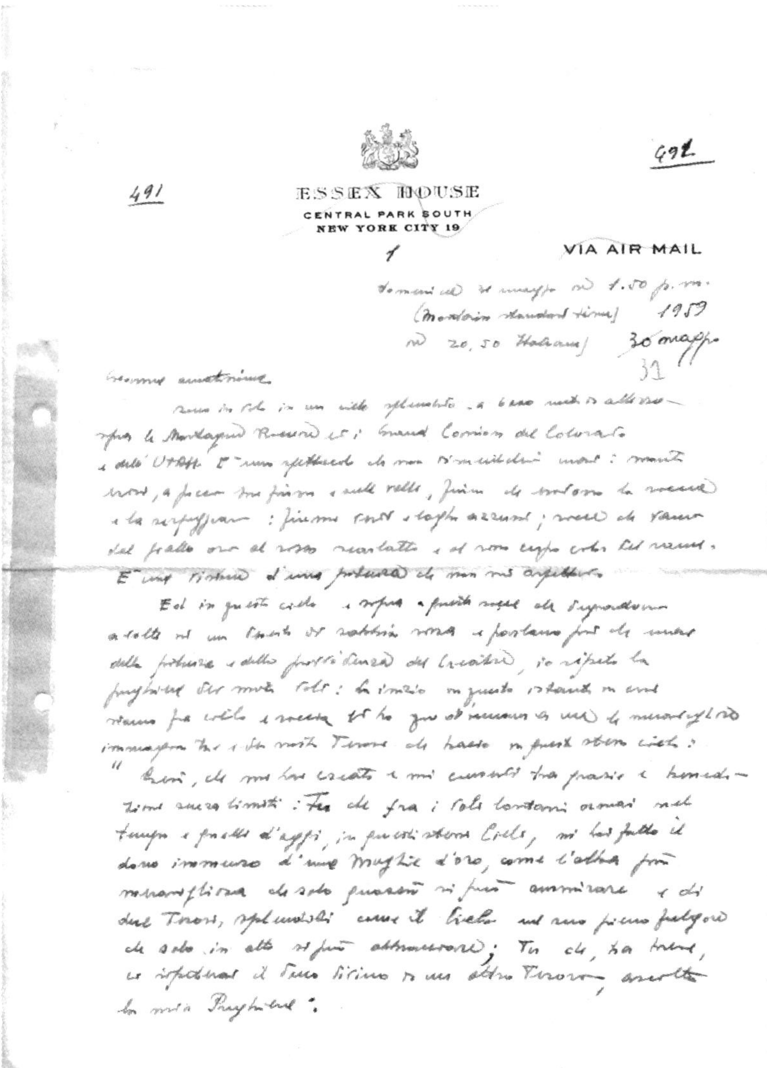

491 ESSEX HOUSE 492

CENTRAL PARK SOUTH
NEW YORK CITY 19

1 VIA AIR MAIL

domenica 31 maggio ore 1.50 p.m.
(Mountain standard time) 1959
ore 20,50 italiane) 30 maggio 31

Gianna amatissima,

sono in volo in un cielo splendido a 6000 metri di altezza sopra le Montagne Rocciose ed i Grand Canyon del Colorado e dell'Utah. È uno spettacolo che non si dimentica mai: monti rossi, a picco, fra fiumi e nelle valli, fiumi che scorrono la roccia e la [illegible]: fiumi verdi e laghi azzurri; rocce che vanno dal giallo oro al rosso scarlatto e al rosso cupo color del sangue. È una visione d'una potenza che non si aspettava.

Ed in questo cielo e sopra a queste rocce che si spandono a volte in un deserto di sabbia rossa e parlano più che mai della potenza e della provvidenza del Creatore, io ripeto la preghiera dei nostri voli: la inizio in questo istante in cui siamo fra cielo e roccia [illegible] ho [illegible] la meravigliosa immagine [illegible] Tesori che [illegible] in questo stesso cielo:

"Gesù, che mi hai creato e mi circondi fra grazie e benedizioni senza limiti: Tu che fra i voli lontani ormai nel tempo e quello d'oggi, in questi stessi Cieli, mi hai fatto il dono immenso d'una Moglie d'oro, come l'alba più meravigliosa che solo quassù si può ammirare e di due Tesori, splendidi come il Cielo nel suo pieno fulgore che solo in alto si può attraversare; Tu che, da tempo, [illegible] il Tuo Divino [illegible] altro Tesoro, ascolta la mia Preghiera".

Letter of Pietro to Gianna, May 31th, 1959. (seen on p. 132)

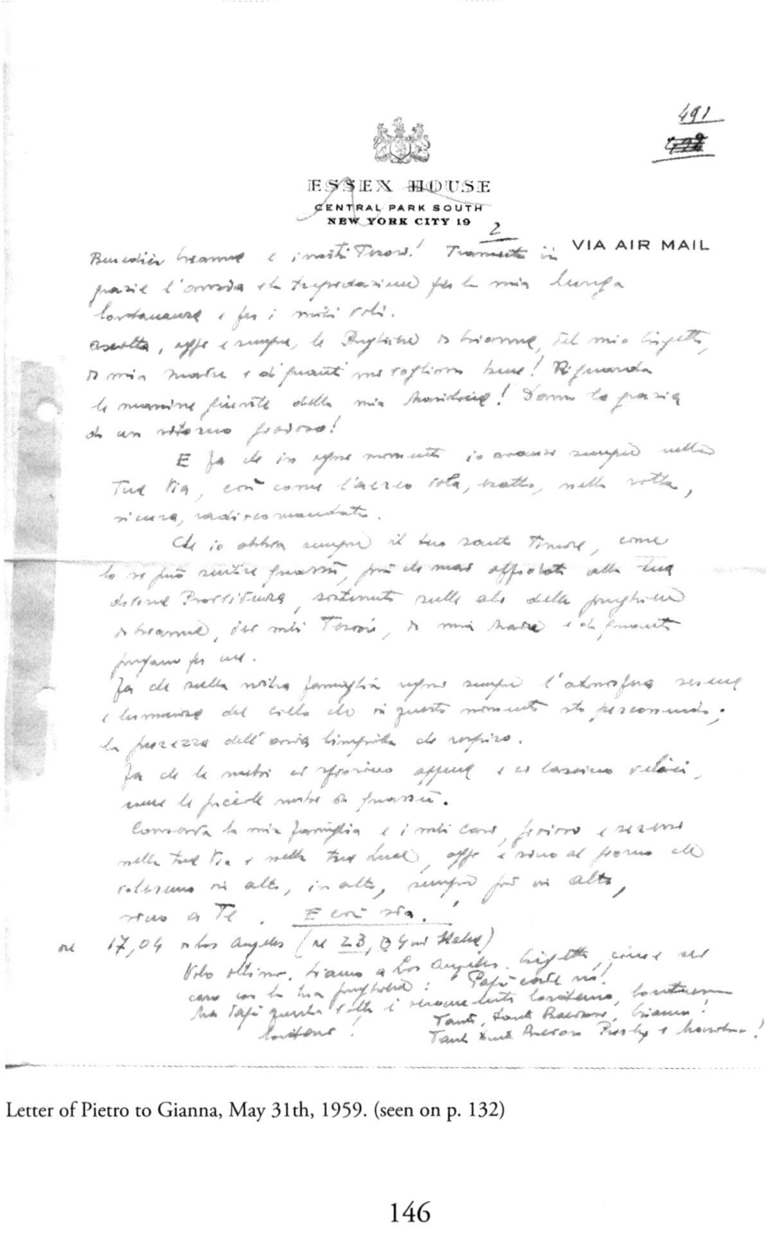
491

ESSEX HOUSE
CENTRAL PARK SOUTH
NEW YORK CITY 19

VIA AIR MAIL

Letter of Pietro to Gianna, May 31th, 1959. (seen on p. 132)